The Quotable

The Quotable

John Adams

Edited and with an Introduction by
RANDY HOWE

THE LYONS PRESS
GUILFORD, CONNECTICUT
An imprint of The Globe Pequot Press

The Lyons Press is an imprint of The Globe Pequot Press.

Cover design by Georgiana Goodwin

Design by Sheryl P. Kober

Library of Congress Cataloging-in-Publication Data is available on file.

ISBN 978-1-59921-409-2

Printed in the United States of America

10 9 8 7 6 5 4 3 2 1

This book is dedicated to my son, David.
I have hopes for you like John had for John Quincy!

A nod of appreciation to Chuck Howe, a research assistant
whose efforts always do wonders for my sanity.
Another nod to Holly Rubino and Ellen Urban:
one brought this project to light and the other showed me
how to move beyond cut and paste to actually be an editor.
A big thanks to all three of you.

Contents

Introduction

> I am but an ordinary Man. The Times alone
> have destined me to Fame . . .
> —From a diary entry, April 26, 1779

If you created a list, in order, of the most important founding fathers, chances are John Adams wouldn't come first. He might not even be the second or third patriot on the list and that's a historical shame.

Of course, it's always a dead heat between George Washington and Thomas Jefferson for the top spot. Thomas Paine and Patrick Henry are probably in your top five, as is Alexander Hamilton. Benjamin Franklin and even George Mason get mention, but nobody in that fab five belongs ahead of John Adams. Even Samuel Adams, with his tasty beer and disdain for highly taxed tea should fall somewhere south of his second cousin. That's because John Adams sacrificed an important chunk of his family life to secure the loans that financed our revolution. That's because he helped write and edit some of the nation's most important documents. That's because he was a vice president, a president, and the father of a president. John Adams might not be the first person who comes to mind when listing the founding fathers, but recent books and a TV miniseries would seem to indicate that this is a patriot whose time has come.

John Adams was born to a fifth generation Massachusetts farmer, and deacon, who hoped his namesake would grow up to become a minister. After attending Harvard, though, Adams entered the profession of law. He put this knowledge to use in a controversial case, defending the British soldiers indicted in the Boston Massacre trial. Perhaps this is why, despite his role in the revolution, King George III welcomed Adams in his court. Of course, Adams was also willing to defend his fellow colonists, as he did in the case of *Rex v. Corbet*, which involved four sailors accused of murdering a British sailor. Truth, justice, and the American way—these things mattered greatly to John Adams.

In the years leading up to the revolution, Adams served his future country by writing in protest of various acts of Parliament and King George and also by attending the first and second Continental Congresses in Philadelphia. During the war, Adams was sent to Europe where he managed to avoid spies and the temptations of foreign riches to ably act as an ambassador. In 1783, he convinced the British to recognize America's autonomy and to sign the Treaty of Paris. Americans wanted independence but also the respect of foreign powers, and Adams was the guy working for it. Shortly after returning to the family and hometown that he loved so much, he was elected the nation's first vice president. As usual, he answered the call, serving in that capacity from 1789 to 1797. The degree of public recognition he had desired for so many years finally came as he was elected president in 1796. From 1797 to 1801, he ably bridged the gap between George Washington and Thomas Jefferson, becoming, in the meanwhile, the first president to live in the White House.

Adams's relationship with Jefferson, in their final years, left a record of reflection that sheds amazing light on the revolution and the first years of the nation. The two founding fathers wrote frequently, providing historians with some of the most valuable letters they could ever hope to get their hands on. Intriguing when they agreed on matters, but downright captivating when they disagreed, a whole book of their correspondences exists and is not superfluous.

John Adams was a patriot and a revolutionary, thus the title of the book's first chapter: "The Fires of Adversity: Adams on Revolution and True Patriotism." Next is "The Die Is Cast: Adams on Conflict and War," followed by "The Divine Science: Adams on Statehood and Politics." Chapter Four, "One Central Truth: Adams on Justice, Freedom, and Federalism," chronicles Adams's various roles as they related to America's transition from colony to country. These roles included attorney in Boston, ambassador abroad, and midwife to the U.S. Constitution. Each position was one of great power and informed his opinions on the dangers of public service; this is the central theme of Chapter Five, "The Jaws of Power: Adams on Self-Interest and the Public Good."

John Adams was a deep thinker and his mind might very well have been wasted had he lived during any other time or in any other nation. He understood politics and he understood people. That is why "By Prejudices and Passions: Adams on His Fellow Man" is included in the book and it's why there are more than fifty quotes and even some observations about individual leaders of that time. Although most of those quotes are complimentary, there is a highly critical side of Adams on display in the chapter titled "Foolish Trumpery: Adams on Religion." Adams's condemnation was born of the great disappointment he felt about organized religion. He knew that religious leaders had the power to do a world of good, but in far too many cases had yet to do so.

He approached everything in a philosophical manner, and in the very first sentence of his biography on the White House Web site, Adams is said to have been "more remarkable as a political philosopher than as a politician." Whatever the case may be, he also had a sense of humor. In "Done with Reflection: Adams as Philosopher and Funny Guy," you will find the second president to be a man full of fun as well as philosophy. It would be remiss to portray him as just another deep thinker in an age of deep thinkers. His dry wit and hints of sarcasm make the idea of spending a night sipping cider by a fire and listening to his stories seem quite appealing. He might have been a man of conviction, but Adams was also a jovial sort, and if jovial is a nice way of saying pleasantly plump, then jovial it is!

John Adams, one of two presidents to see his son take office, struggled mightily to come to terms with his role as father and ambassador. Often taken away from his wife and children, he understood that the fledgling nation needed a paternal presence in Europe and went willingly. However, the quotes included here make obvious just how difficult it was for him to be away from his native Braintree, Massachusetts. In reading Adams's letters and diary entries, the difficulty and danger of a transatlantic journey are made undeniably real. To sail across the North Sea in winter is not something Adams would wish upon his worst enemy, and his words show why. A sympathetic heart might also break when considering that a letter penned in December might not arrive home to Abigail until June——if at all. Adams had tremendous pride in his children and tremendous love for his wife, and no examination of our second president could be complete without giving Abigail her proper due. All can be found in "All My Hopes: Adams as a Family Man" and "Your Benign Influence: In the Words of Abigail Adams."

Finally, in "America's First Ambassador: About John Adams" there is a concentration of quotations from others to describe this collection's hero. Included at the end are several quotes proving that nobody understood John Adams better than John Adams. His introspection makes for engaging reading as do his sharp eye, keen mind, and commanding prose. In quotes by him, and in quotes about him, an important tale is told not just that of John Adams and his family, but of a country that was teetering on the precipice in its formative years: implosion and invasion on one side, superpower status on the other. John Adams's story is so intertwined with the history of the United States that to read his words, and those of his family and peers, is to read the story of a colony that, against all odds, became a nation. If not for his deep thought and expansive writing, the country might not have been able to break free from Great Britain and the world would be bereft of so many wonderful quotations. Thomas Jefferson called Adams the "Colossus of Independence" and fortunately for us, he was also a colossus of the written word.

The phrase "founding father" should be synonymous with the name John Adams, just as it is for George Washington and Thomas Jefferson. Nobody sacrificed more for his country. Nobody left a more vibrant legacy for historians and history buffs to pore over.

One

THE FIRES OF ADVERSITY:
ADAMS ON REVOLUTION AND
TRUE PATRIOTISM

In 1774, during a time of martial law government, General Thomas Gage was named royal governor of Massachusetts because of his extensive military experience. Clearly, the British wanted to squash the colonial protests with a heavy-handed approach. It was Gage who ordered Samuel Adams and John Hancock arrested, and it was a Gage-ordered raid that led to Paul Revere's ride. The Sons of Liberty were watching carefully his every move; this was a time for rebels to become revolutionaries.

Before Gage could disband the General Court, John Adams and four others were elected to represent Massachusetts at the Continental Congress. Rather than a call to arms, the delegates put their heads together. One reason the revolution succeeded is that it was led by rational thinkers. This was an organized effort, supported by the majority of colonists.

As evidence of this, the same men who started the revolution were still in power when the war ended. They were even still in power when the government was put in place! And Adams is an exemplar of this public support and subsequent staying power.

Even though he was more of a diplomat than a soldier, it would be a mistake to undervalue Adams's abilities as both a rebel and a patriot. At a crucial moment in our nation's history, he argued for the colonies to declare their independence from Great Britain, and at a crucial juncture in the Revolutionary War, he acted on his own, traveling to Amsterdam to secure much needed loans from the Dutch. This money, not easy to come by when backed by nothing more than America's lowly credit and the promises of a man many considered a radical, provided a much-needed boost to the war effort.

Adams had begun his rebellious ways by publicly taking a stance not many would have predicted. For one, he was no fan of Thomas Paine and his famous pamphlet, *Common Sense*. He was also willing to defend British soldiers who'd shot colonists in the Boston Massacre. He used his knowledge of the law to fight for what was right and he used his pen—or quill, if you will—to state the case for independence. Adams helped draft the *Declaration of Rights and Grievances*, and it was Adams who knew that the people of Massachusetts could not fight the British on their own. Adams knew that Southern support for the rebellion was essential and that having a Virginian at the helm might help toward this end. And so, he squelched his urge to pen the *Declaration of Independence*, and recommended that Thomas Jefferson write it. Adams was of a similar mindset when rather than pushing hard for his own presidency, he supported George Washington. This is why Adams is deserving of the name "patriot."

In 1775 Major General William Howe was put in charge of the British forces and General Gage returned home. Once in England, he pulled no punches, reporting that only a very large force could be expected to quell the rebellion and even recommending that foreign troops be hired to aid in the effort. Adams and his fellow Americans had gotten their message across, loud and clear.

At the first Continental Congress, which convened in October of 1774, John Adams was the main author of the *Declaration of Rights and Grievances* which was the precursor to, and foundation of, the *Declaration of Independence*. The Congress also decided to enforce an embargo of trade with Great Britain and called for the raising of a colonial militia.

People and nations are forged in the fires of

adversity.

Resistance to sudden violence, for the preservation not only of my person, my limbs, and life, but of my property, is an indisputable right of nature which I have never surrendered to the public by the compact of society, and which perhaps, I could not surrender if I would.

—From the *Boston Gazette*, September 5, 1763

I always consider the settlement of America with reverence and wonder, as the opening of a grand scene and design in providence, for the illumination of the ignorant and the emancipation of the slavish part of mankind all over the earth.

—In *Dissertation on the Canon and the Feudal Law*, from the *Boston Gazette,* August 1765

We are now concluding the Year 1765, tomorrow is the last day, of a Year in which America has shewn such Magnanimity and Spirit, as never before appeared, in any Country for such a Tract of Country. And Wednesday will open upon Us a new Year 1766, which I hope will procure Us, innumerable Testimonies from Europe in our favour and Applause, and which we all hope will produce the greatest and most extensive joy ever felt in America, on the Repeal both of the stamp Act and sugar Act, at least of the former.

—From a diary entry, December 30, 1765

You say that at the time of the Congress, in 1765, "The great mass of the people were zealous in the cause of America." "The great mass of the people" is an expression that deserves analysis. New York and Pennsylvania were so nearly divided, if their propensity was not against us, that if New England on one side and Virginia on the other had not kept them in awe, they would have joined the British. Marshall, in his life of Washington, tells us, that the southern States were nearly equally divided. Look into the Journals of Congress, and you will see how seditious, how near rebellion were several counties of New York, and how much trouble we had to compose them.

—DESCRIBING THE STRUGGLES OF CREATING A UNIFIED FRONT
IN A LETTER TO THOMAS McKEAN, AUGUST 31, 1813

We are now upon the Beginning of a Year of greater Expectation than any, that has passed before it. This Year brings Ruin or Salvation to the British Colonies. The Eyes of all America, are fixed on the [British] Parliament. In short Britain and America are staring at each other. — And they will probably stare more and more for sometime.

—From a diary entry, January 1, 1766

There are but two sorts of men in the world, freemen and slaves. The very definition of a freeman is one who is bound by no law to which he has not consented. Americans would have no way of giving or withholding their consent to the acts of this parliament, therefore they would not be freemen.

*We live, my dear soul,
in an age of trial.
What will be the consequence,
I know not.*

—In a letter to Abigail, 1774

It *is true*, that the people of this country in general, and of this province in special, have a hereditary apprehension of and aversion to lordships, temporal and spiritual. Their ancestors fled to this wilderness to avoid them; they suffered sufficiently under them in England. And there are few of the present generation who have not been warned of the danger of them by their fathers or grandfathers, and enjoined to oppose them.

—*From* Novanglus, *February 13, 1775*

I have said, that the practice of free governments alone can be quoted with propriety to show the sense of nations. But the sense and practice of nations is not enough. Their practice must be reasonable, just, and right, or it will not govern Americans.

—From *Novanglus*, March 6, 1775

◈

*T*he practice of nations has been different. The Greeks planted colonies, and neither demanded nor pretended any authority over them; but they became distinct, independent commonwealths. The Romans continued their colonies under the jurisdiction of the mother commonwealth; but, nevertheless, they allowed them the privileges of cities. Indeed, that sagacious city seems to have been aware of difficulties similar to those under which Great Britain is now laboring. She seems to have been sensible of the impossibility of keeping colonies planted at great distances, under the absolute control of her senatus-consulta.

—From *Novanglus*, March 6, 1775

*I*f the English parliament were to govern us, where did they get the right, without our consent, to take the Scottish parliament into a participation of the government over us? When this was done, was the American share of the democracy of the constitution consulted? If not, were not the Americans deprived of the benefit of the democratical part of the constitution? And is not the democracy as essential to the English constitution as the monarchy or aristocracy?

—From *Novanglus*, March 6, 1775

*S*o that our ancestors, when they emigrated, having obtained permission of the king to come here, and being never commanded to return into the realm, had a clear right to have erected in this wilderness a British constitution, or a perfect democracy, or any other form of government they saw fit. They, indeed, while they lived, could not have taken arms against the King of England, without violating their allegiance; but their children would not have been born within the king's allegiance, would not have been natural subjects, and consequently not entitled to protection, or bound to the king.

—From *Novanglus*, March 6, 1775

A cts of parliament have been passed to annex Wales, &c. &c. to the realm; but none ever passed to annex America. But if New England was annexed to the realm of England, how came she annexed to the realm of, or kingdom of Great Britain? The two realms of England and Scotland were, by the act of union, incorporated into one kingdom, by the name of Great Britain; but there is not one word about America in that act.

—From *Novanglus*, March 6, 1775

*T*his people, under great trials and dangers, have discovered great abilities and virtues, and that nothing is so terrible to them as the loss of their liberties. If these arts and violences are persisted in, and still greater, concerted and carried on against them, the world will see that their fortitude, patience, and magnanimity will rise in proportion.

—From *Novanglus*, March 6, 1775

*S*uch events as the resistance to the Stamp Act, and to the Tea Act, particularly the destruction of that which was sent by the ministry, in the name of the East India Company, have ever been cautiously spoken of by the whigs, because they knew the delicacy of the subject, and they lived in continual hopes of a speedy restoration of liberty and peace. But we are now thrown into a situation, which would render any further delicacy upon this point criminal.

—From *Novanglus*, March 6, 1775

But America is a great, unwieldy Body. Its Progress must be slow. It is like a large Fleet sailing under Convoy. The fleetest Sailors must wait for the dullest and slowest. Like a Coach and six—the swiftest Horses must be slackened and the slowest quickened, that all may keep an even Pace.

*—In a letter to Abigail,
June 11 and June 17, 1775*

Now, let me ask you, if the Parliament of Great Britain had all the natural foundations of authority, wisdom, goodness, justice, power, in as great perfection as they ever existed in any body of men since Adam's fall; and if the English nation was the most virtuous, pure, and free that ever was; would not such an unlimited subjection of three millions of people to that parliament, at three thousand miles distance, be real slavery?

The national debt, before the last war, was near a hundred millions. Surely America had no share in running into that debt. What is the reason, then, that she should pay it? . . . What is the reason that the Massachusetts has paid its debt, and the British minister, in thirteen years of peace, has paid none of his?

The resolves of the house of burgesses of Virginia upon the Stamp Act did great honor to that province, and to the eminent patriot, Patrick Henry, who composed them. But these resolves made no alteration in the opinion of the colonies, concerning the right of parliament to make that act.

In the Year 1773 arose a Controversy

concerning the Independence of the Judges. The King had granted a Salary to the judges of our Superiour Court and forbidden them to receive their Salaries as usual from the Grants of the House of Representatives, and the Council and Governor, as had been practiced till this time. This as the judges Commissions were during pleasure made them entirely dependent on the Crown for Bread [as] well as office.

—From *The Adams Papers: Diary and Autobiography of John Adams*

The Second Day of July 1776, will be the most memorable Epocha, in the History of America. I am apt to believe that it will be celebrated, by succeeding generations, as the great anniversary festival. It ought to be commemorated, as the Day of Deliverance by solemn acts of devotion to God Almighty. It ought to be solemnized with pomp and parade, with shews, games, sports, guns, bells, bonfires and illuminations from one end of this Continent to the other from this time forward forever more.

—In a letter to Abigail, July 3, 1776

I am well aware of the Toil and Blood and Treasure, that it will cost us to maintain this Declaration, and support and defend these States. Yet through all the Gloom I can see the Rays of ravishing Light and Glory. I can see that the End is more than worth all the Means. And that Posterity will triumph in that Days Transaction, even although We should rue it, which I trust in God We shall not.

—In a letter to Abigail, July 3, 1776

Every Colony, upon the Continent will soon be in the same Situation. They are erecting Governments, as fast as Children build Cobb Houses. But I conjecture they will hardly throw them down again, so soon.

—In a letter to Abigail, July 7, 1776

I believed that too many commercial Projects and private Speculations were in contemplation by the composition of those Committees: but even those had not contributed so much to it, as the great division in the House on the Subject of Independence and the mode of carrying on the War.

—From *The Adams Papers: Diary and Autobiography of John Adams*

The Revolution was effected before the war commenced. The Revolution was in the hearts and minds of the people…. This radical change in the principles, opinions, sentiments, and affections of the people, was the real American Revolution.

—From a letter to Hezekiah Niles, February 13, 1818

Adams's feelings

about the Tories who remained loyal to King George III.

I on my part, may, perhaps, in a course of papers, penetrate arcana too; show the wicked policy of the tories; trace their plan from its first rude sketches to its present complete draught; show that it has been much longer in contemplation than is generally known, who were the first in it their views, motives, and secret springs of action, and the means they have employed.

*I*t will clearly appear, who were the aggressors, and who have acted on the defensive from first to last; who are still struggling, at the expense of their ease, health, peace, wealth, and preferment, against the encroachments of the tories on their country, and who are determined to continue struggling, at much greater hazards still, and, like the Prince of Orange, are resolved never to see its entire subjection to arbitrary power, but rather to die fighting against it in the last ditch.

◈

I have heretofore intimated my intention of pursuing the tories through all their dark intrigues and wicked machinations, and to show the rise and progress of their schemes for enslaving this country.

◈

*T*here is nothing in this world so excellent that it may not be abused. The abuses of the press are notorious. It is much to be desired, that writers on all sides would be more careful of truth and decency; but, upon the most impartial estimate, the tories will be found to have been the least so of any party among us.

◈

*W*e were about one third Tories, and [one] third timid, and one third true blue.

◈

*P*owder and artillery are the most efficacious, sure and infallible conciliatory measures we can adopt.

—Writing in response to Tories and others who felt reconciliation with Great Britain was still an option, 1776

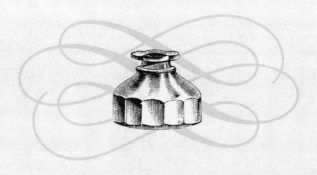

from Adams's autobiography on Thomas Paine and *Common Sense*.

*I*n the Course of this Winter appeared a Phenomenon in Philadelphia a Star of Disaster Disastrous Meteor, I mean Thomas Paine.

◆

*H*e . . . gleaned from those he saw the common place Arguments concerning Independence: such as the Necessity of Independence, at some time or other, the peculiar fitness at this time: the justice of it: the Provocation to it: the necessity of it: our Ability to maintain it &c. &c. Dr. Rush put him upon Writing on the Subject, furnished him with the Arguments which had been urged in Congress an hundred times, and gave him his title of common Sense.

*H*is Arguments from the old Testiment, were ridiculous, but whether they proceeded from honest Ignorance, and or foolish [Superstition] on one hand, or from willfull Sophistry and knavish Hypocricy on the other I know not. The other third part relative to a form of Government I considered as flowing from simple Ignorance, and a mere desire to please the democratic Party in Philadelphia, at whose head were Mr. Matlock, Mr. Cannon and Dr. Young.

◆

I regretted however, to see so foolish a plan recommended to the People of the United States, who were all waiting only for the Countenance of Congress, to institute their State Governments. I dreaded the Effect so popular a pamphlet might have, among the People, and determined to do all in my Power, to counter Act the Effect of it.

◆

I answered that *the die was now cast*; I had passed the Rubicon. Swim or sink, live or die, survive or perish with my country was my unalterable determination.

—Describing a conversation with Jonathan Sewall, the last British attorney general of Massachusetts, 1774

The thought that we might be driven to the sad necessity of breaking our connection with Great Britain, exclusive of the carnage and destruction which it was easy to see must attend the separation, always gave me a great deal of grief.

—In a letter to Abigail, 1776

Although the Opposition was still inveterate, many Members of Congress began to hear me with more Patience, and some began to ask me civil questions. How can the People institute Governments? My Answer was by Conventions of Representatives, freely, fairly and proportionally chosen.

—FROM *THE ADAMS PAPERS: DIARY AND AUTOBIOGRAPHY OF JOHN ADAMS*

My Letters, instead of being destroyed, fell into the hands of the Ennemy, and [were] immediately printed, with a little garbling. They thought them a great Prize. The Ideas of Independence, to be sure were glaring enough, and they thought they should produce quarrells among the Members of Congress, and a division of the Colonies. Me they expected utterly to ruin because, as they represented, I had explicitly avowed my designs of Independence. I cared nothing for this. I had made no secret in or out of Congress of my Opinion that Independence was become indispensable; and I was perfectly sure, that in a little time the whole Continent would be of my Mind.

—From *The Papers: Diary and Autobiography of John Adams*

Sink or swim, live or die, survive or perish, I am with my country from this day on. You may depend on it.

—From a letter to a friend, 1774

There is a new, and a grand Scene open before me—a Congress. This will be an assembly of the wisest Men upon the Continent, who are Americans in Principle, i.e. against the Taxation of Americans, by Authority of Parliament.

—From a diary entry, dated June 20, 1774

You and I. . . have been sent into life at a time when the greatest lawgivers of antiquity would have wished to live. How few of the human race have ever enjoyed an opportunity of making an election of government, more than of air, soil, or climate, for themselves or their children! When, before the present epoch, had three millions of people full power and a fair opportunity to form and establish the wisest and happiest government that human wisdom can contrive?

—From *Thoughts on Government,* 1776

Before God, I believe the hour has come. My judgement approves this measure, and my whole heart is in it. All that I have, and all that I am, and all that I hope in this life, I am now ready here to stake upon it. And I leave off as I began, that live or die, survive or perish, I am for the Declaration. It is my living sentiment, and by the blessing of God it shall be my dying sentiment.

—FROM A DIARY ENTRY, JULY 1, 1776

Independence now,
and Independence for ever!

—From a diary entry, July 1, 1776

To say you will trade with all the World, deserves Consideration. I have not absolutely discarded every Glimpse of a Hope of Reconciliation. Our Prospect is gloomy. I cant agree, that We shall not export our own Produce. We must treat with foreign Nations upon Trade. They must protect and support Us with their Fleets. When you once offer your Trade to foreign Nations, away with all Hopes of Reconciliation.

—From a diary entry about the debates
in the Continental Congress, October 3, 1776

Will the Cause suffer much, if this Preamble is not published at this Time? If the Resolve is published without the Preamble. The Preamble contains a Reflection upon the Conduct of some People in America. It was equally irreconcileable to good Conscience Nine Months ago, to take the Oaths of Allegiance, as it is now.

*—From a diary entry about the debates
in the Continental Congress, May 13-15, 1776*

Before the final Question was put, the new Delegates from New Jersey came in, and Mr. Stockton, one of them Dr. Witherspoon and Mr. Hopkinson, very respectable Characters, expressed a great desire to hear the Arguments. All was Silence: No one would speak: all Eyes were turned upon me. . . I summed up the Reasons, Objections and Answers, in as concise a manner as I could, till at length the Jersey Gentlemen said they were fully satisfied and ready for the Question, which was then put and determined in the Affirmative.

—Recalling the Continental Congress debate over declaring independence

Mr. Dickinson… had prepared himself apparently with great Labour and ardent Zeal, and in a Speech of great Length, and all his Eloquence, he combined together all that had before been written in Pamphlets and News papers and all that had from time to time been said in Congress by himself and others. He conducted the debate, not only with great Ingenuity and Eloquence, but with equal Politeness and Candour: and was answered in the same Spirit.

—Recalling the Continental Congress debate over declaring independence (John Dickinson, of Pennsylvania, was in favor of negotiating with King George III and against declaring independence)

The Committee of whom I was one requested me to draught a resolve which I did and by their Direction reported it. Opposition was made to it, and Mr. Duane called it a Machine to fabricate independence but on the 15th of May 1776 it passed. It was indeed on all hands considered by Men of Understanding as equivalent to a declaration of Independence: tho a formal declaration of it was still opposed by Mr. Dickinson and his Party.

—From *The Adams Papers: Diary and Autobiography of John Adams*

I began by saying that *this was the first time* of my Life that I had ever wished for the Talents and Eloquence of the ancient Orators of Greece and Rome, for I was very sure that none of them ever had before him a question of more Importance to his Country and to the World.

—Recalling the Continental Congress debate
over declaring independence

I have reasons to believe that no colony which shall assume a government under the people, will give it up.

—IN A LETTER TO ABIGAIL, MAY 1776

But we should always remember that a free constitution of civil government cannot be purchased at too dear a rate, as there is nothing on this side of Jerusalem of equal importance to mankind.

—In a letter to Archibald Bulloch,
July 1, 1776

Objects of the most stupendous magnitude, measures in which the lives and liberties of millions, born and unborn are most essentially interested, are now before us. We are in the very midst of revolution, the most complete, unexpected, and remarkable of any in the history of the world.

—Addressing the Continental Congress before the vote for independence was taken, July 1, 1776

I am well aware of the *toil and blood and treasure* that it will cost to maintain this Declaration, and support and defend these States. Yet through all the gloom I can see the rays of ravishing light and glory. I can see that the end is worth more than the means.

—In a letter to Abigail, July 3, 1776

August 1, 1776, diary entry about the debates in the Continental Congress.

*W*e loose an equal Representation. We represent the People. It will tend to keep up colonial Distinctions. We are now a new Nation.

❖

*T*he more a Man aims at serving America the more he serves his Colony.

❖

*T*he Q.[uestion] is whether we must have Trade or not. We can't do without Trade. We must have Trade. It is prudent not to put Virtue to too serious a Test. I would use American Virtue, as sparingly as possible lest We wear it out.

—From a diary entry about the debates in the Continental Congress, October 5, 1776

❖

Yesterday the greatest question was decided which ever was debated in America; and a greater perhaps never was, nor will be, decided among men. A resolution was passed without one dissenting colony, "that these United Colonies are, and of right ought to be, free and independent States."

—In a letter to Abigail, July 3, 1776

The truth is that neither then nor at any former time, since I had attained my maturity in Age, Reading and reflection had I imbibed any general Prejudice against Kings, or in favour of them. It appeared to me then as it has done ever since, that there is a State of Society in which a Republican Government is the best, and in America the only one.

—FROM *THE ADAMS PAPERS: DIARY AND AUTOBIOGRAPHY OF JOHN ADAMS*

America has been the *sport*
of European wars and politics
long enough.

—In a letter to Congress, from Europe,
April 18, 1780

*Huzza for the new world
and farewell to the old one.*

—In a letter to Thomas Jefferson,
December 6, 1787

It is with pleasure that I have learned your design to write upon the American Revolution... But I hope, sir, you will not accuse me of presumption, of affectation, or of singularity, if I venture to express my opinion, that it is yet too soon to undertake a complete history of that great event; and that there is no man, either in America or Europe, at this day, capable of performing it, or who is in possession of the materials requisite and necessary for that purpose.

—From a letter to the Abbè de Mably, included in the appendix of the *Defence of the Constitutions of Government of the United States of America*, 1787

The United States of America have exhibited, perhaps, the first example of governments erected on the simple principles of nature; and if men are now sufficiently enlightened to disabuse themselves of artifice, imposture, hypocrisy, and superstition, they will consider this event as an era in their history.

—From *A Defence of the Constitutions of Government of the United States of America*, 1787

When the Convention has fabricated a Government, or a Constitution rather, how do We know the People will submit to it? If there is any doubt of that, the Convention may send out their Project of a Constitution, to the People in their several Towns, Counties or districts, and the People may make the Acceptance of it their own Act.

—Describing how the U.S. Constitution might come to be accepted by the American people

Never since I *was born* was America so happy as at this time.

—Describing life in 1790

It was a Station of too much responsibility and danger in the times and Circumstances in which We lived and were destined to live.

—FROM *THE ADAMS PAPERS: DIARY AND AUTOBIOGRAPHY OF JOHN ADAMS*, RESPONDING TO JOHN JAY WHEN ASKED ABOUT SERVING AS THE VICE PRESIDENT

Employed in the service of my country abroad during the whole course of these transactions, I first saw the Constitution of the United States in a foreign country. Irritated by no literary altercation, animated by no public debate, heated by no party animosity, I read it with great satisfaction, as the result of good heads prompted by good hearts, as an experiment better adapted to the genius, character, situation, and relations of this nation and country than any which had ever been proposed or suggested.

—INAUGURAL ADDRESS, MARCH 4, 1794

A trust of the greatest magnitude is committed to this legislature and the eyes of the world are upon you.

—Addressing the nation's first Senate, 1797

While other states are desolated with foreign war or convulsed with intestine divisions, the United States present the pleasing prospect of a nation governed by mild and equal laws, generally satisfied with the possession of their rights, neither envying the advantages nor fearing the power of other nations, solicitous only for the maintenance of order and justice and the preservation of liberty, increasing daily in their attachment to a system of government in proportion to their experience of its utility, yielding a ready and general obedience to laws flowing from the reason and resting on the only solid foundation—the affections of the people.

—Special Address to the Senate and the House,
May 16, 1797

It *is not large,* in the first place. It is but the farm of a patriot.

—Describing his home in Braintree

During the Second Continental Congress, John Adams made clear that the *Declaration of Independence* was necessary but that the formation of constitutions by each state was far more important. To this end, in 1776 he published his pamphlet, *Thoughts on Government*, which had a significant influence on individual states and the writing of their constitutions.

Two

THE DIE IS CAST:
ADAMS ON CONFLICT AND WAR

John Adams was never a soldier. Nonetheless, he was a warrior to be reckoned with. He was never an officer, either. Nonetheless, he was one of the people most responsible for financing the U.S. military in its fight against the British. Adams waged war with his words, whether they were inflammatory or conciliatory, and he won battles with his sales skills. Without funding, after all, an army can't buy bullets. Or, in this case, musket balls. But long before the revolution, Adams was putting his skills to use, fighting for the cause with wisdom and words.

Governor Francis Bernard, the royally appointed governor of Massachusetts, requested help from the British government after the Stamp Act was passed and they sent the *H.M.S. Romney* straight to Boston Harbor. Adams showed that the pen can indeed be mightier than the sword, writing the letter from the Committee on Correspondence that listed the colonists' complaints. The Committee did not like Parliament's approach to managing the colonies, and Adams summed up why they felt their rights were being infringed upon.

British soldiers drilled in front of Adams's residence in Boston, and with each passing day it became more and more clear that the Red Coats had no plans of backing off. Governor Bernard recognized what an important, influential man Adams was and decided to offer him the post of Attorney General of Massachusetts, but Adams was smarter, and more dedicated, than that. He understood that Bernard planned on completely suppressing the colonists and with this gesture was hoping to get rid of one of his adversaries. Friends close, enemies closer . . . But Adams could not be bought. Soon thereafter, Governor Bernard was forced out of office by the civil unrest, and it was the first of many victories for the Sons of Liberty and patriots like John Adams.

Adams understood the danger of civil unrest and worked to minimize it in the United States. Years later, he would comment on the French Revolution, warning that it was bloody to the extreme and that this would accomplish little other than sowing the seeds for future violence. This ability to see the big picture, coupled with his skills of negotiation, made him widely respected as a diplomat. Particular to war was his ability to trace its roots back to human nature, national pride, and the basic economics of trade. As vice president, and then president, Adams worked to improve his country's standing in the eyes of the world without stepping on too many international toes. He hoped to achieve respect with diplomacy rather than brute strength. He would readily choose compromise over conflict every time.

As president, Americans let Adams know that they preferred war to diplomacy by voting him out of office in 1800, but history has been more kind. The quotations that follow demonstrate why.

On May 10, 1775, Fort Ticonderoga was captured by Ethan Allen and the Green Mountain Boys and the Second Continental Congress began meeting in Philadelphia. One month later, John Adams nominated George Washington to lead the new nation's armed forces. After all, Washington was the only man to attend the Continental Congress in full military dress! In addition to Washington's post, the Congress also approved ten companies of riflemen to join the American forces already located in Boston.

The die is cast. The people have passed the river and cut away the bridge.

—Writing after the Boston Tea Party,
December 1773

My heart bled for the poor *People of Boston*, imprisoned within the Walls of their City by a British Army, and We knew not to what Plunder or Massacres or Cruelties they might be exposed.

—FROM *THE ADAMS PAPERS: DIARY AND
AUTOBIOGRAPHY OF JOHN ADAMS*

The Colonies are now much more warlike and powerfull than they were, during the last War. A martial Spirit has seized all the Colonies. They are much improved in Skill and Discipline. They have now a large standing Army. They have many good officers. They abound in Provisions.

—From a diary entry, March 1, 1776

We are obliged to go fair, and softly, and in Practice you know We are the subjects. We have only the Name of Masters, and rather than give up this, which would compleatly subject Us to the Despotism of the Peticoat, I hope General Washington, and all our brave Heroes would fight.

—In a letter to Abigail, April 14, 1776

This is a revolution, dammit!
We're going to have to offend somebody!

—During the debates over declaring independence,
1776

The present State of Things requires *Reconciliation*, or Means to carry on War. Intelligence We must have. We must have Powder and Shot. We must support the Credit of our Money.

—From a diary entry

You must have a Navy to carry on the War. You can't have a Navy Says the Gentleman. What is the Consequence? I say, that We must submit.

—From a diary entry about the debates in the Continental Congress, October 21, 1776

The object is great which *We have in View*, and We must expect a great expense of blood to obtain it.

—IN A LETTER TO ARCHIBALD BULLOCH,
JULY 1, 1776

Adams's descriptions of life during war in diary entries dated September 15 and 16, 1777.

We live in critical Moments! Mr. Howes Army is at Middleton and Concord. Mr. Washingtons, upon the Western Banks of Schuylkill, a few Miles from him. I saw this Morning an excellent Chart of the Schuylkill, Chester River, the Brandywine, and this whole Country, among the Pensilvania Files. This City is the Stake, for which the Game is playd. I think, there is a Chance for saving it, although the Probability is against Us.

❖

Mr. Howe I conjecture is waiting for his Ships to come into the Delaware. Will W. [Washington] attack him? I hope so — and God grant him Success.

No Newspaper this Morning. Mr. Dunlap has moved or packed up his Types. A Note from G. Dickinson that the Enemy in N. Jersey are 4000 strong. Howe is about 15 miles from Us, the other Way. The City seems to be asleep, or dead, and the whole State scarce alive. Maryland and Delaware the same.

◆

The Prospect is chilling, on every Side. Gloomy, dark, melancholly, and dispiriting. When and where will the light spring up?

◆

From whence is our Deliverance to come? Or is it not to come? Is Philadelphia to be lost? If lost, is the Cause lost? No—the Cause is not lost—but it may be hurt.

◆

I seldom regard Reports, but it is said that How[e] has marked his Course, from Elke, with Depredation. His Troops have plunderd Henroosts, dairy Rooms, the furniture of Houses and all the Cattle of the Country. The Inhabitants, most of whom are Quakers, are angry and disappointed, because they were promised the Security of their Property.

◈

H ow is the Interest of France and Spain affected, by the dispute between B.[Britain] and the C. [Colonies]? Is it the Interest of France [to] stand neuter, to join with B. or to join with the C. Is it not her Interest, to dismember the B. Empire? Will her Dominions be safe, if B. and A. [America] remain connected?

—From a diary entry, March 1, 1776

◈

Be *it remembered, then,* that there are tumults, seditions, popular commotions, insurrections, and civil wars, upon just occasions as well as unjust.

I have many reasons to think that not one of them, not even Spain or France, wishes to see America rise very fast to power. We ought therefore to be cautious how we magnify our ideas and exaggerate our expressions of the generosity and magnanimity of any of these powers.

—In a letter to Congress, describing the
European powers, April 18, 1780

A navy is our natural and only defense.

—In a letter to Congress,
1780

Reasoning has been all lost. Passion, prejudice, interest, necessity have governed and will govern; and a century must roll away before any permanent and quiet system will be established.

—In a letter to Thomas Jefferson, regarding the violence of the French Revolution, 1793

As it is often necessary that nations should treat for the mutual advantage of their affairs, and especially to accommodate and terminate differences, and as they can treat only by ministers, the right of embassy is well known and established by the law and usage of nations. The refusal on the part of France to receive our minister is, then, the denial of a right; but the refusal to receive him until we have acceded to their demands without discussion and without investigation is to treat us neither as allies nor as friends, nor as a sovereign state.

—Special Address to the Senate and the House,
May 16, 1797

The naval establishment must occur to every man who considers the injuries committed on our commerce, the insults offered to our citizens, and the description of vessels by which these abuses have been practiced. As the sufferings of our mercantile and seafaring citizens can not be ascribed to the omission of duties demandable, considering the neutral situation of our country, they are to be attributed to the hope of impunity arising from a supposed inability on our part to afford protection. To resist the consequences of such impressions on the minds of foreign nations and to guard against the degradation and servility which they must finally stamp on the American character is an important duty of Government.

—Special Address to the Senate and the House,
May 16, 1797

The national defense must be provided for as well as the support of Government; but both should be accomplished as much as possible by immediate taxes, and as little as possible by loans.

—STATE OF THE UNION ADDRESS, NOVEMBER 12, 1797

I have transmitted these papers to Congress not so much for the purpose of communicating an account of so daring a violation of the territory of the United States as to show the propriety and necessity of enabling the Executive authority of Government to take measures for protecting the citizens of the United States and such foreigners as have a right to enjoy their peace and the protection of their laws within their limits in that as well as some other harbors which are equally exposed.

—ADDRESS TO THE SENATE AND HOUSE, FEBRUARY 5, 1798

The law of France enacted in January

last, which subjects to capture and condemnation neutral vessels and their cargoes if any portion of the latter are of British fabric or produce, although the entire property belong to neutrals, instead of being rescinded has lately received a confirmation by the failure of a proposition for its repeal. While this law, which is an unequivocal act of war on the commerce of the nations it attacks, continues in force those nations can see in the French Government only a power regardless of their essential rights, of their independence and sovereignty; and if they possess the means they can reconcile nothing with their interest and honor but a firm resistance.

—State of the Union Address,
December 8, 1798

In making to you this declaration I give a pledge to France and the world that the Executive authority of this country still adheres to the humane and pacific policy which has invariably governed its proceedings, in conformity with the wishes of the other branches of the Government and of the people of the United States.

—State of the Union Address, December 8, 1798

Perhaps no country ever experienced more sudden and remarkable advantages from any measure of policy than we have derived from the arming for our maritime protection and defense.

—State of the Union Address, December 8, 1798

The present Navy of the United States, called suddenly into existence by a great national exigency, has raised us in our own esteem, and by the protection afforded to our commerce has effected to the extent of our expectations the objects for which it was created.

—State of the Union Address, November 22, 1800

He may long continue to live and be well; and to see the good work of the War prospering in his hands; for a more necessary War, was never undertaken. It is necessary against England; necessary to convince France that we are something: and above all necessary to convince ourselves, that we are not, Nothing.

—COMMENTING ON JAMES MADISON AND THE WAR OF 1812,
IN A LETTER TO BENJAMIN RUSH, OCTOBER 8, 1813

As to the history of the revolution, my ideas may be peculiar perhaps singular. What do we mean by the revolution? The war? That was no part of the revolution; it was only an effect and consequence of it. The revolution was in the minds of the people, and this was effected from 1760 to 1775, in the course of fifteen years, before a drop of blood was shed at Lexington.

—IN A LETTER TO THOMAS JEFFERSON, AUGUST 24, 1815

Great is the guilt of an unnecessary war.

—In a letter to Abigail, describing the pressure
to go to war with the French

During the war, John Adams worked hard to gain public support from the Dutch people, reminding them at every chance that The Netherlands was a republic that, just like the United States, had to win its independence. In 1782, The Netherlands recognized the United States as a country and Adams as its ambassador, and in 2007, Dutch-American Friendship Day was declared to celebrate 225 years of alliance.

Three

THE DIVINE SCIENCE:
ADAMS ON STATEHOOD AND POLITICS

After signing the Declaration of Independence, the Continental Congress asked John Adams to develop a framework for the nation's new government. When he agreed to do so, it was official: his transition from rebel to politician was underway.

While drafting his Plan of 1776, Adams was also busy figuring out how to avoid war with Great Britain. This was not to be and while trying to negotiate peace with a British admiral on Staten Island, the Continental Congress voted to send Adams to France. There, he would serve as an emissary of peace and good will. Translation: he was to make sure that the French remained America's allies in the war against their common enemy. By the time he arrived, Benjamin Franklin had already won over the French, so Adams ventured to The Netherlands, where he scored a major loan to help finance the revolution. Adams later returned to obtain a second loan and his legacy as a statesman and a politician was set in stone.

Adams held the idea of serving as a politician in high regard. He wrote, "Politics are the divine science, after all." If one was to serve as a politician, Adams believed, he must be a man of convictions. Certainly, if he were to view the nonpartisan fence sitters of modern times, he would cringe with disappointment. To General Horatio Gates, he wrote, "In politics the middle way is none at all." This idea he handed down to his son, John Quincy Adams, who decided to go against his fellow Federalists in support of Thomas Jefferson. He boldly stated, "The president has recommended the measure on his high responsibility. I would not consider, I would not deliberate; I would act!" Apparently, Adams men were not intent on being mere party men. They were bent on acting upon their convictions and doing what was best for the United States.

To avoid that safe middle ground is to risk making enemies. It should be no surprise to learn then that, oftentimes, Adams did not have the support of a majority of Americans. In this regard, he was perhaps a better statesman than politician. After all, Adams served just one term as president, losing to Thomas Jefferson in 1800. He was able to navigate the waters of international diplomacy with great skill, however. When the war between France and Great Britain threatened the commercial growth of the United States, Adams stepped in and negotiated with the French, even though this was an unpopular position. Many Americans, as well as the French, underestimated Adams, mistaking his accommodating nature for gullibility and weakness. When the French called for a bribe from American commissioners in the "X, Y, Z Affair," Adams was fit to be tied. More than anything, he wanted respect for his country from the world's superpowers. In his subtle way, he demanded it. The American people appreciated his pride, and Adams's popularity was once again on the rise. His reputation as a statesman and a politician was rising, too.

In serving as an ambassador to Europe, John Adams crossed the Atlantic four times and traveled more than 29,000 miles, more than any other American politician of his time.

If Aristotle, Livy, and Harrington knew what a republic was, the British constitution is much more like a republic than an empire. They define a republic to be a government of laws, and not of men. If this definition is just, the British constitution is nothing more or less than a republic, in which the king is first magistrate. This office being hereditary, and being possessed of such ample and splendid prerogatives, is no objection to the government's being a republic, as long as it is bound by fixed laws, which the people have a voice in making, and a right to defend.

—Writing in the *Boston Gazette*,
March 6, 1775

of the Continental Congress in 1776.

Three Committees were appointed, One for preparing a Declaration of Independence, another for reporting a Plan of a Treaty to be proposed to France, and a third to digest a System of Articles of Confederation to be proposed to the States. I was appointed on the Committee of Independence, and on that for preparing the form of a Treaty with France: on the Committee of Confederation Mr. Samuel Adams was appointed.

My time is too totally filled from the moment I get out of bed until I return to it, [with] visits, ceremonies, company, business, newspapers, pamphlets, etc.

—In a letter to Abigail

*C*an't we oblige B. [Britain] to keep a Navy on foot the Expence of which will be double to what they will take from Us. I have heard of Bullion Sp. [Spanish] Flotas being stoppd least they should be taken — But perishable Commodities never were stopped. Opressing Open your Ports to Foreigners. Your Trade will become of so much Consequence, that Foreigners will protect you... I think the Merchants ought to judge for themselves of the danger and Risque. We should be blamed if We did not leave it to them.

—From a diary entry,
February 16, 1776

Reason first—You are a Virginian, and a Virginian ought to appear at the head of this business. Reason second—I am obnoxious, suspected, and unpopular. You are very much otherwise. Reason third—You can write ten times better than I can.

—In a letter to Thomas Jefferson, explaining why Jefferson should write the ***Declaration of Independence***

describing the dangers
of ocean travel.

No Man could keep upon his Legs, and nothing could be kept in its Place — an universal Wreck of every Thing in all Parts of the Ship, Chests, Casks, Bottles &c. No Place or Person was dry. On one of these Nights, a Thunder bolt struck 3 Men upon deck and wounded one of them a little, by a Scorch upon his Shoulder. It also struck our Main Topmast.

—February 21, 1778

The Life I lead is a dull Scaene to me. No Business; No Pleasure; No Study... Our little World is all wet and damp: there is nothing I can eat or drink without nauseating. We have no Spirits for Conversation, nor any Thing to converse about. We see nothing but Sky, Clouds and Sea, and then Seas, Clouds and Sky.

—March 3, 1778

❖

I have often heard of learning a Language as French or English on the Passage, but I believe very little of any Thing was ever learned on a Passage. There must be more Health and better Accommodations.

—March 3, 1778

❖

W henever I arrive at any Port in Europe, whether in Spain or France, my first Enquiry should be concerning the Designs of the Enemy.—What Force they

mean to send to America? Where they are to obtain Men?
. . . What the Condition of their Finances? What the State
of their Armies, but especially of their Fleets. What No.
of Ships they have fitted for the Sea—what their Names,
Number of Men and Guns, weight of Metal &c.—where they
lie? &c. The Probability or Improbability of a War, and the
Causes and Reasons for and against each supposition.

—From a diary entry, March 5, 1778

❖

We then saw another Vessell, chased and came
up with her which proved to be a French Brig
from Marseilles to Nantes. This last cost Us very dear. Mr.
Barrons our 1st Lt. attempting to fire a Gun, as a signal to
the Brig, the Gun burst, and tore the right Leg of this excellent Officer, in Pieces, so that the Dr. was obliged to ampu-
tate it, just below the Knee. I was present at this affecting
Scaene and held Mr. Barron in my Arms while the Doctor

put on the Turnequett and cutt off the Limb. Mr. Barrons
bore it with great Fortitude and Magnanimity.

—Describing an officer who had lost his leg
when cannon backfired, March 14, 1778

M y principal Motive for omitting to keep a
regular and particular Journal, has been
the Danger of falling into the Hands of my Enemies, and
an Apprehension that I should not have an Opportunity of
destroying these Papers in such a Case.

—March 20, 1778

I should have been pleased to have kept a minute
Journal of all that passed, in the late Chases and
turbulent Weather, but I was so wet, and every Thing and
Place was so wett—every Table and Chair was so wrecked
that it was impossible to touch a Pen, or Paper.

—February 24, 1778

Adams's interactions
with and observations of, the French in 1778 and 1779.

I was then shewn the Palace of Versailles, and happened to be present when the King passed through, to Council. His Majesty seeing my Colleagues, graciously smiled, and passed on. I was then shewn the Galleries, and Royal Apartments, and the K's bedchamber. The Magnificence of these Scaenes, is immense. The Statues, the Paintings, the every Thing is sublime.

—From a diary entry, April 11, 1778

◈

I t is with much Grief and Concern that I have learned from my first landing in France, the Disputes between the Americans, in this Kingdom . . . Parties and Divisions among the Americans here, must have disagreable if not pernicious Effects.

—From a diary entry, April 21, 1778

*T*hat if they, and their Representatives in America, were determined to countenance and support by their Influence such Men and Measures in America, it was no matter how soon the Alliance was broke. That no Evil could be greater, nor any Government worse, than the Toleration of such Conduct.

—Commenting on the French in a diary entry,
February 8, 1779

*W*hen I arrived in France, the French Nation had a great many Questions to settle.

The first was—Whether I was the famous Adams, Le fameux Adams? Ah, le fameux Adams?

—From a diary entry, February 11, 1779

*I*t must be further known, that altho the Pamphlet Common sense, was received in France and in all Europe with Rapture: yet there were certain Parts of it, that they did not choose to publish in France. The Reasons of this, any Man may guess. Common sense undertakes to prove, that Monarchy is unlawful by the old Testament. They therefore gave the Substance of it, as they said, and paying many Compliments to Mr. Adams, his sense and rich Imagination, they were obliged to ascribe some Parts to Republican Zeal.

—Describing the misunderstanding, in France,
that he was the author of *Common Sense*, 1779

I *have no security* that every letter I write will not be broken open and copied and transmitted to Congress and the English newspapers. They would find no treason or deceit in them, it is true, but they would find weakness and indiscretion, which they would make ill use of.

—In a letter to Abigail,
explaining the distant tone
of his letters from France,
1779

On

Adams's diplomatic efforts with the Dutch.

*I*t may not . . . be amiss to hint that the central situation of this country, her extensive navigation, her possessions in the East and West Indies, the intelligence of her merchants, the number of her capitalists, and the riches of her funds, render a connection with her very desirable to America.

*T*his is the Anniversary of the Battle of Lexington, and of my Reception at the Hague, by their High Mightinesses. This last Event is considered by the Historians, and other Writers and Politicians of England and France as of no Consequence: and Congress and the Citizens of the United States in General concur with them in Sentiment. There is nothing I dread so much as a division of the Republic into two great parties, each arranged under its leader and converting measures in opposition to each other.

—From a diary entry, written in London, April 19, 1786

[I]t shall be the duty of legislators and magistrates... to encourage private societies and public institutions, rewards and immunities for the promotion of agriculture, arts, sciences, commerce, trades, manufactures, and a natural history of the country; to countenance and inculcate the principles of humanity and general benevolence, public and private charity, industry and frugality, honesty and punctuality in their dealings, sincerity, good humor, and all social affections and generous sentiments among the people.

—From Section 2 of *The Constitution of the Commonwealth of Massachusetts,* 1780

You are apprehensive of foreign Interference, Intrigue, Influence. So am I.—But, as often as Elections happen, the danger of foreign Influence recurs. The less frequently they happen the less danger.—And if the Same Man may be chosen again, it is probable he will be, and the danger of foreign Influence will be less. Foreigners, seeing little Prospect will have less Courage for Enterprize.

—In a letter to Thomas Jefferson, December 6, 1787

written to Samuel Adams,
dated October 18, 1789.

All good government is and must be republican.

◆

$\mathcal{A}$re we not, my friend, in danger of rendering the word republican unpopular in this country by an indiscreet, indeterminate, and equivocal use of it? Whenever I use the word republic with approbation, I mean a government in which the people have collectively, or by representation, an essential share in the sovereignty . . . the republican forms in Poland and Venice are much worse, and those of Holland and Bern very little better, than the monarchical form in France before the late revolution.

◆

My fundamental maxim of government is
never to trust the lamb to the wolf.

—Writing about the revolution in France

From Adams's discourse
**with friend, physician, patriot, and abolitionist
Benjamin Rush, dated 1789.**

I am a mortal and irreconcilable enemy to monarchy.

The continent is a kind of whispering gallery and acts and speeches are reverberated around from New York in all directions. The report is very loud at a distance when the whisper is very gentle in the center.

On the trepidation

Adams felt in his role as the nation's first vice president.

I am Not wholly without experience in public
assemblies, I have been more accustomed to take
a share in their debates than to preside in their deliberations.

◆

entlemen, I feel a great difficulty how to act. I am
Vice President. In this I am nothing, but I may be
everything.

◆

Whether I should say, "Mr. Washington," "Mr. President," "Sir," may it please your excellency," or what else? I observed that it had been common while he commanded the army to call him "His Excellency," but I was free to own it would appear to me better to give him no title but "Sir" or "Mr. President," than to put him on a level with a governor of Bermuda.

—Asking the Senate's advice in creating a title
for President George Washington, 1789

If national pride is ever justifiable or excusable it is when it springs, not from power or riches, grandeur or glory, but from conviction of national innocence, information and benevolence.

—Inaugural Address, March 4, 1797

Gentlemen of the Senate and Gentlemen of the House of Representatives: We are met together at a most interesting period. The situation of the principal powers of Europe are singular and portentous. Connected with some by treaties and with all by commerce, no important event there can be indifferent to us.

—State of the Union Address, November 12, 1797

It *is interest alone* which does it and it is interest alone which can be trusted.

—In an address to Congress,
discussing the decisions
of foreign nations

Whenever the channels of diplomatical communication between the United States and France shall be opened, I shall demand satisfaction for the insult and reparation for the injury.

—*Address to the Senate and House,*
February 5, 1798

I think it my duty to invite the Legislature of the Union to examine the expediency of establishing suitable regulations in aid of the health laws of the respective States; for these being formed on the idea that contagious sickness may be communicated through the channels of commerce, there seems to be a necessity that Congress, who alone can regulate trade, should frame a system which, while it may tend to preserve the general health, may be compatible with the interests of commerce and the safety of the revenue.

—State of the Union Address, December 8, 1798

Always disposed and *ready to embrace* every plausible appearance of probability of preserving or restoring tranquility, I nominate William Vans Murray, our minister resident at The Hague, to be minister plenipotentiary of the United States to the French Republic.

—ANNOUNCING THE APPOINTMENT OF AN AMBASSADOR TO FRANCE AND, IN TURN, THE AVOIDANCE OF WAR, FEBRUARY 18, 1799

The act of Congress relative to the seat of the Government of the United States requiring that on the 1st Monday of December next it should be transferred from Philadelphia to the District chosen for its permanent seat, it is proper for me to inform you that the commissioners appointed to provide suitable buildings for the accommodation of Congress and of the President and of the public offices of the Government have made a report of the state of the buildings designed for those purposes in the city of Washington, from which they conclude that the removal of the seat of Government to that place at the time required will be practicable and the accommodation satisfactory.

—State of the Union Address, December 3, 1799

John Adams was the president responsible for the first-ever State of the Union Address delivered in Washington, D.C. He gave his speech on November 22, 1800.

If, turning our eyes homeward, we find reason to rejoice at the prospect which presents itself; if we perceive the interior of our country prosperous, free, and happy; if all enjoy in safety, under the protection of laws emanating only from the general will, the fruits of their own labor, we ought to fortify and cling to those institutions which have been the source of such real felicity and resist with unabating perseverance the progress of those dangerous innovations which may diminish their influence.

—State of the Union Address, November 22, 1800

I can not omit once more to recommend to your serious consideration the judiciary system of the United States. No subject is more interesting than this to the public happiness, and to none can those improvements which may have been suggested by experience be more beneficially applied.

—State of the Union Address, November 22, 1800

As one of the grand community of nations, our attention is irresistibly drawn to the important scenes which surround us. If they have exhibited an uncommon portion of calamity, it is the province of humanity to deplore and of wisdom to avoid the causes which may have produced it.

—STATE OF THE UNION ADDRESS, NOVEMBER 22, 1800

The science of government it is my duty to study, more than all other sciences; the arts of legislation and administration and negotiation ought to take the place of, indeed exclude, in a manner, all other arts.

—In a letter to Abigail, dated 1780

Although it would have been more conformable to my own judgment and inclination to have agreed to that instrument unconditionally, yet as in this point I found I had the misfortune to differ in opinion from so high a constitutional authority as the Senate, I judged it more consistent with the honor and interest of the United States to ratify it under the conditions prescribed than not at all.

—Address to the Senate regarding Ratification of the Convention with France, March 2, 1801

Our obligations to our country never cease but with our lives.

—In a letter to Benjamin Rush, April 18, 1808

It is probable that our difference of opinion may in some measure be produced by a difference of character in those among whom we live. From what I have seen of Massachusetts and Connecticut myself, and still more from what I have heard, and the character given of the former by yourself, who know them so much better, there seems to be in those two states a traditionary reverence for certain families, which has rendered the offices of the government nearly hereditary in those families.

—In a letter from Thomas Jefferson, October 28, 1813

You surprise me with the account you give of the strength of family distinction still existing in your State. With us it is so totally extinguished, that not a spark of it is to be found but lurking in the hearts of some of our old tories; but all bigotries hang to one another, and this in the Eastern States hangs, as I suspect, to that of the priesthood. Here youth, beauty, mind and manners, are more valued than a pedigree.

—In a letter from Thomas Jefferson, January 24, 1814

If there is ever an *amelioration of the condition* of mankind, philosophers, theologians, legislators, politicians and moralists will find that the regulation of the press is the most difficult, dangerous and important problem they have to resolve. Mankind cannot now be governed without it, nor at present with it.

—In a letter to James Lord, February 11, 1815

Abuse of words has been the great instrument of sophistry and chicanery, of party, faction, and division of society.

—In a letter to J. H. Tiffany, March 31, 1819

There are persons whom in my heart I despise, others I abhor. Yet I am not obliged to inform the one of my contempt, nor the other of my detestation. This kind of dissimulation . . . is a necessary branch of wisdom, and so far from being immoral . . . that it is duty and a virtue.

—In a diary entry, describing the need for this kind of self-discipline in politics and business

In 1797, when John Adams was sworn in as the second president, the population of the United States was 5,308,483. Vermont, Kentucky, and Tennessee had recently joined the Union so that there were now sixteen states.

Four

ONE CENTRAL TRUTH:
ADAMS ON JUSTICE, FREEDOM,
AND FEDERALISM

While working in France with Thomas Jefferson, Adams wrote *A Defence of the Constitutions of Government of the United States.* Published in 1787, this three-volume set was an opportunity to share his theories on constitutional law. From the foundation laid out in Adams's work, revolutionary Americans took their leap of faith. The book also stands as a milestone in Adams's progression as a champion of democracy and freedom.

At times, Adams was foolishly accused of being an aristocrat when, in fact, nobody was more anti-monarchy and pro-democracy. He was, for example, one of the first of the founding fathers to champion the idea of trial by jury. There were even fewer American leaders willing to stand up against slavery. Adams did so, arguing that it should be outlawed in the U.S.

Constitution. To Adams, liberty was not just a concept, but a practice. In the end, though, his political instincts won out. As one of the editors of the document, he agreed to cut the phrase that would have made the slave trade illegal. His opponent in the debate was Thomas Jefferson—he believed Southern states would not ratify this version of the Constitution—and the two would discuss what they had done, and why, for the rest of their lives.

There were other issues available for them to debate in their letters. The concept of freedom was easy to understand, but not necessarily easy to guarantee. The concept of a democratic government was the goal, but how to attain it, and protect it against political misdeeds consumed much of their time. John Adams was happy to put his time into this kind of dialogue. Whether discussing the issues with other founding fathers or bouncing ideas off of Abigail, in everything he did Adams proved that he cared deeply about democracy, freedom, and the government of the United States.

The Constitution of the Commonwealth of Massachusetts was written by John Adams, Samuel Adams, and James Bowdoin. It was adopted in 1780 and is the oldest continuous constitution in the world. John Adams was the politician responsible for calling Massachusetts a "commonwealth" rather than a state, and he did so because he wished to follow the example of Virginia.

I shall have liberty to think for myself without molesting others or being molested myself.

—In a letter to brother-in-law Richard Cranch,
August 29, 1756

From
Dissertation on the Canon and the Feudal Law,
featured in the *Boston Gazette*,
August 1765.

❖

*B*e not intimidated, therefore, by any terrors, from publishing with the utmost freedom whatever can be warranted by the laws of your country; nor suffer yourselves to be wheedled out of your liberty by any pretenses of politeness, delicacy, or decency. These, as they are often used, are but three different names for hypocrisy, chicanery, and cowardice.

❖

*L*iberty cannot be preserved without a general knowledge among the people.

*S*et before us the conduct of our own British ancestors, who defended for us the inherent rights of mankind against foreign and domestic tyrants and usurpers, against arbitrary kings and cruel priests; in short against the gates of earth and hell.

*B*ut none of the means of information are more sacred, or have been cherished with more tenderness and care by the settlers of America, than the press. Care has been taken that the art of printing should be encouraged, and that it should be easy and cheap and safe for any person to communicate his thoughts to the public.

Were I to define the British constitution, therefore, I should say it is a limited monarchy, or a mixture of the three forms of government commonly known in the schools... And it is [the] reservation of fundamentals, of the right of giving instructions, and of new elections, which creates a popular check, upon the whole government which alone secures the constitution from becoming an aristocracy, or a mixture of monarchy and aristocracy only.

—From the *Boston Gazette*, January 27, 1766

We often hear in Conversation Doctrines advanced for Law, which if true, would render juries a mere Ostentation and Pagentry and the Court absolute judges of Law and It cannot therefore be an unseasonable Speculation to examine into the real Powers and Duties of Juries, both in Civil and Criminal Cases, and to discover the Boundary the important Boundary between the Power of the Court and that of the jury, both in Points of Law and of Fact.

—From a diary entry, February 12, 1771

It is not only the trial juror's right, but his duty, to find the verdict according to his own best understanding, judgment and conscience, though in direct opposition to the direction of the court.

Adams recalls his role

in defending the British soldiers in the Boston Massacre trial of 1770, taken from his diary and court records.

The part I took in defense of Cptn. Preston and the Soldiers, procured me anxiety, and obloquy enough. It was, however, one of the most gallant, generous, manly and disinterested actions of my whole life, and one of the best pieces of service I ever rendered my country.

Judgement of death against those soldiers would have been as foul a stain upon this country as the executions of the Quakers or Witches, anciently. As the evidence was, the verdict of the jury was exactly right.

The law, in all vicissitudes of government, fluctuations of the passions, or flights of enthusiasm, will preserve a steady undeviating course; it will not bend to the uncertain wishes, imaginations, and wanton tempers of men.

—From his summation in *Rex v Wemms*

I devoted myself to endless labour and Anxiety if not to infamy and death, and that for nothing, except, what indeed was and ought to be all in all, a sense of duty.

—From a diary entry dated March 5, 1773
(the three year anniversary of Boston Massacre)

*B*efore or after the Tryal, Preston sent me ten Guineas and at the Tryal of the Soldiers afterwards Eight Guineas more, which were . . . all the pecuniary Reward I ever had for fourteen or fifteen days labour, in the most exhausting and fatiguing Causes I ever tried: for hazarding a Popularity very general and very hardly earned: and for incurring a Clamour and popular Suspicions and prejudices, which are not yet worn out and never will be forgotten as long as History of this Period is read.

—From a diary entry dated March 5, 1773

This however is no Reason why the Town should not call the Action of that Night a Massacre, nor is it any Argument in favour of the Governor or Minister, who caused them to be sent here. But it is the strongest Proofs of the Danger of Standing Armies.

—From a diary entry dated March 5, 1773

As the happiness of the people is the sole end of government, so the consent of the people is the only foundation of it, in reason, morality, and the natural fitness of things.

—From a Proclamation adopted by the
Council of Massachusetts Bay, 1774

a unicameral legislation and argues in favor of a three-branch government in *Thoughts on Government*, 1775.

I think a people cannot be long free, nor ever happy, whose government is in one assembly.

◆

*N*o good government but what is republican . . . the very definition of a republic is "an empire of laws, and not of men."

◆

A single assembly is liable to all the vices, follies, and frailties of an individual; subject to fits of humor, starts of passion, flights of enthusiasm, partialities, or prejudice, and consequently productive of hasty results and absurd judgments. And all these errors ought to be corrected and defects supplied by some controlling power.

❖

A single assembly is apt to grow ambitious, and after a time will not hesitate to vote itself perpetual.

❖

A representative assembly is still less qualified for the judicial power, because it is too numerous, too slow, and too little skilled in the laws.

❖

B ecause a single assembly, possessed of all the powers of government, would make arbitrary laws for their own interest, execute all laws arbitrarily for their own interest, and adjudge all controversies in their own favor.

From a letter
**written to James Sullivan,
May 26, 1776.**

*I*t is certain in Theory, that the only moral Foundation of Government is the Consent of the People, But to what an Extent Shall We carry this Principle? Shall We Say, that every Individual of the Community, old and young, male and female, as well as rich and poor, must consent, expressly to every Act of Legislation?

❖

*W*hence arises the Right of the Majority to govern, and the Obligation of the Minority to obey? from Necessity, you will Say, because there can be no other Rule.

❖

Statesmen, my dear Sir, may plan and speculate for liberty, but it is religion and morality alone, which can establish the principles upon which freedom can securely stand. The only foundation of a free Constitution is pure virtue, and if this cannot be inspired into our People in a greater Measure than they have it now, they may change their rulers and the forms of government, but they will not obtain a lasting liberty.

—In a letter to Zabdiel Adams, June 21, 1776

The people, when they have been unchecked, have been as unjust, tyrannical, brutal, barbarous, and cruel, as any king or senate possessed of uncontrollable power. The majority has eternally, and without one exception, usurped over the rights of the minority.

From

Adams's Thoughts on Government, 1776.

*L*aws for the liberal education of youth, especially of the lower class of people, are so extremely wise and useful, that, to a humane and generous mind, no expense for this purpose would be thought extravagant.

◈

*T*he dignity and stability of government in all its branches, the morals of the people, and every blessing of society depend so much upon an upright and skillful administration of justice, that the judicial power ought to be distinct from both the legislative and executive, and independent upon both, that so it may be a check upon both, as both should be checks upon that.

◈

*T*he judges, therefore, should be always men of learning and experience in the laws, of exemplary morals, great patience, calmness, coolness, and attention.

◈

The people must erect the whole Building
with their own hands upon the broadest foundation.
That this could be done only by conventions of
representatives chosen by the People . . .

—Commenting on Massachusetts and
the state's Constitutional Convention in 1779

*The right of a nation to kill a tyrant in case
of necessity can no more be doubted than to hang
a robber, or kill a flea.*

—From the *Constitution of Massachusetts:*
Declaration of Rights, 1780

Adams placed on the executive branch.

*I*f there is one central truth to be collected from the history of all ages, it is this: that the people's rights and liberties, and the democratical mixture in a constitution, can never be preserved without a strong executive, or, in other words, without separating the executive from the legislative power.

❖

*I*f the executive power, or any considerable part of it, is left in the hands of an aristocratical or democratical assembly, it will corrupt the legislature as necessarily as rust corrupts iron, or as arsenic poisons the human body; and when the legislature is corrupted, the people are undone.

❖

We should begin by setting conscience free. When all men of all religions . . . shall enjoy equal liberty, property, and an equal chance for honors and power . . . we may expect that improvements will be made in the human character and the state of society.

—In a letter to Dr. Price, April 8, 1785

You are the afraid of the one—I, of the few. We agree perfectly that the many should have a full fair and perfect Representation.—You are Apprehensive of Monarchy; I, of Aristocracy. I would therefore have given more Power to the President and less to the Senate.

—In a letter to Thomas Jefferson, December 6, 1787

You are apprehensive the President when once chosen, will be chosen again and again as long as he lives. So much the better as it appears to me.

—In a letter to Thomas Jefferson, December 6, 1787

What think you of a Declaration of Rights? Should not such a thing have preceded the model?

—In a letter to Thomas Jefferson, 1787

From

A Defence of the Constitutions
of Government of the United States
# of America, 1787.

*C*hildren should be educated and instructed in the principles of freedom.

◆

*T*he rich, the well-born, and the able, acquire an influence among the people that will soon be too much for simple honesty and plain sense, in a house of representatives. The most illustrious of them must, there-fore, be separated from the mass, and placed by them-selves in a senate; this is, to all honest and useful intents, an ostracism.

$\mathcal{T}$he proposition that the people are the best keepers of their own liberties is not true. They are the worst conceivable, they are no keepers at all; they can neither judge, act, think, or will, as a political body.

❖

$\mathcal{A}$mong every people and in every species of republics, we have constantly found a first magistrate, a head, a chief, under various denominations, indeed, and with different degrees of authority...

❖

$\mathcal{T}$o suppose arms in the hands of citizens, to be used at individual discretion, except in private self-defense, or by partial orders of towns, countries or districts of a state, is to demolish every constitution, and lay the laws prostrate, so that liberty can be enjoyed by no man; it is a dissolution of the government. The fundamental law of the militia is, that it be created, directed and commanded by the laws, and ever for the support of the laws.

❖

Thirteen governments [of the original states] thus founded on the natural authority of the people alone, without a pretence of miracle or mystery, and which are destined to spread over the northern part of that whole quarter of the globe, are a great point gained in favor of the rights of mankind.

❖

The new government has my best wishes and most fervent prayers for its success and prosperity; but whether I shall have anything more to do with it, besides praying for it, depends on the future suffrage of freemen.

—Making clear, in a letter to Thomas Jefferson, his desire for the vice presidency, 1788

On Adams's hopes and concerns
for the French Revolution.

*T*he French Revolution will, I hope, produce effects in favor of liberty, equity, and humanity as extensive as this whole globe and as lasting as all time.

—From a letter to Francis van der Kemp

◆

*E*verything will be pulled down. So much seems certain. But what will be built up? Are there any principles of political architecture? . . . Will the struggle in Europe be anything other than a change in impostors?

—From a letter to Samuel Adams

◆

I am no friend to hereditary limited monarchy in America. Do not, therefore, my friend, misunderstand me and misrepresent me to posterity.

—In conversation with Benjamin Rush, 1789

In the first place, what is your definition of republic? Mine is this: A government whose sovereignty is vested in more than one person.

—In a letter to Roger Sherman, July 17, 1789

There must be, however, more employment for the press in favor of the government than there has been, or the sour, angry, peevish, fretful, lying paragraphs which assail it on every side will make an impression on many weak and ignorant people.

—Discussing newspaper coverage of the new government

A Maxim, that all Government originates from the People. We are the Servants of the People sent here to act under a delegated Authority. If we exceed it, voluntarily, We deserve neither Excuse nor justification.

From letters

written in favor of federalism.

*T*he only way to keep us from setting up for ourselves is to disunite us.

—In a letter to Nathan Webb, October 12, 1755

◆

*T*he fate of this government depends absolutely upon raising it above the state governments.

—In a letter to William Tudor

◆

You *have rights antecedent* to all earthly governments: rights that cannot be repealed or restrained by human laws; rights derived from the Great Legislator of the universe.

The essence of a free government consists in an effectual control of rivalries.

—From *Discourse on Davila*, 1790

Inaugural Address,
March 4, 1794.

Returning to the bosom of my country after a painful separation from it for ten years, I had the honor to be elected to a station under the new order of things, and I have repeatedly laid myself under the most serious obligations to support the Constitution. The operation of it has equaled the most sanguine expectations of its friends, and from an habitual attention to it, satisfaction in its administration, and delight in its effects upon the peace, order, prosperity, and happiness of the nation I have acquired an habitual attachment to it and veneration for it.

◆

$\mathcal{W}$e should be unfaithful to ourselves if we should ever lose sight of the danger to our liberties if anything partial or extraneous should infect the purity of our free, fair, virtuous, and independent elections. If an election is to be determined by a majority of a single vote, and that can be procured by a party through artifice or corruption, the Government may be the choice of a party for its own ends, not of the nation for the national good.

We have no government armed with power capable of contending with human passions unbridled by morality and religion. Avarice, ambition, revenge, or gallantry, would break the strongest cords of our Constitution as a whale goes through a net. Our Constitution was made only for a moral and religious people. It is wholly inadequate to the government of any other.

—FROM A MILITARY ADDRESS, OCTOBER 11, 1798

On the one hand, the laws should be executed; on the other, individuals should be guarded from oppression. Neither of these objects is sufficiently assured under the present organization of the judicial department. I therefore earnestly recommend the subject to your serious consideration.

—*State of the Union Address, December 3, 1799*

Checks and Ballances, Jefferson, however you and your Party may have derided them, are our only Security, for the progress of Mind, as well as the Security of Body. Every Species of these Christians would persecute Deists, as soon as either Sect would persecute another, if it had unchecked and unballanced Power. Nay, the Deists would persecute Christians, and Atheists would persecute Deists, with as unrelenting Cruelty, as any Christians would persecute them or one another. Know thyself, human Nature!"

—In a letter to Thomas Jefferson, June 25, 1813

Now I will avow, that I then believe, and now believe, that those general Principles of Christianity, are as eternal and immutable, as the Existence and Attributes of God; and that those Principles of liberty, are as unalterable as human Nature and our terrestrial, mundane System.

—From a diary entry, June 28, 1813

There is but one element of government, and that is THE PEOPLE. From this element spring all governments. "For a nation to be free, it is only necessary that she wills it." For a nation to be slave, it is only necessary that she wills it.

—IN A LETTER TO JOHN TAYLOR, UNITED STATES SENATOR FROM VIRGINIA, 1814

When people talk of the *freedom* of writing, speaking, or thinking, I cannot choose but laugh. No such thing ever existed. No such thing now exists; but I hope it will exist. But it must be hundreds of years after you and I shall write and speak no more.

—In a letter to Thomas Jefferson, 1818

I *would define liberty* to be a power to do as we would be done by. The definition of liberty to be the power of doing whatever the law permits, meaning the civil laws, does not seem satisfactory.

—In a letter to J. H. Tiffany, March 31, 1819

We think ourselves possessed, or, at least, we boast that we are so, of liberty of conscience on all subjects, and of the right of free inquiry and private judgment in all cases, and yet how far are we from these exalted privileges in fact!

—In one of his last letters to Thomas Jefferson, January 23, 1825

On

Adams's position on slavery.

Negro slavery is an evil of colossal magnitude.
—From a letter to Abigail, 1819

◈

*I*t is wrong to admit into the Constitution the idea
that there can be property in man.

◈

*T*he turpitude, the inhumanity, the cruelty, and
the infamy of the African commerce in slaves
have been so impressively represented to the public by the
highest powers of eloquence that nothing that I can say
would increase the just odium in which it is and ought to
be held. Every measure of prudence, therefore, ought to be
assumed for the eventual total extirpation of slavery from
the United States.

—From a letter to Robert J. Evans, June 8, 1819

In his inaugural address, delivered on May 4, 1797 at Philadelphia's Federal Hall, John Adams included a sentence that was 727 words long! The speech itself was 2,318 words long and demonstrated Adams's intention to wholeheartedly support the Constitution, the election process, and relations with France. Adams delivered his speech in Philadelphia, at Federal Hall, before a joint session of Congress.

Five

THE JAWS OF POWER:
ADAMS ON SELF-INTEREST
AND THE PUBLIC GOOD

O n par with power, property, and wealth, greed stands as a theme of this chapter. Even before the Revolutionary War was won, some Americans were putting personal gain ahead of the cause of their country. This bothered John Adams to no end.

"They worry one another like mastiffs," he wrote. "Scrambling for rank and pay like apes for nuts." This was his description not of members of Parliament nor of elected officials, but of American officers. Adam couldn't believe that these men would entertain such thoughts during the fight for independence—already, self-interest was permeating the dream and souring it into a nightmare. Still, he did understand the importance of compensation.

When the founding fathers began to discuss the government and those who would run it, the idea of serving without pay was supported by George Washington and Benjamin Franklin. It was John Adams who pointed out that this would guarantee a government of the wealthy and *for* the wealthy. And by his own admission, he had personal reasons for wanting to attach a salary to positions like president and vice president. John Adams was not an independently wealthy man.

Looking at the bigger picture, though, Adams knew what an impact wealth and property could have. A burgeoning democracy could very easily turn into an aristocracy if the founding fathers weren't careful. Adams was all for capitalism, but reminded his fellow countrymen that, "The balance of power in a society accompanies the balance of property in land." He also warned that, "Power always thinks it has a great soul and vast views beyond the comprehension of the weak." Adams understood that the government could not last if certain segments of society, whether they were weak (i.e., poor) or wealthy, felt unrepresented. After all, Great Britain had just learned that lesson the hard way.

> As president, Adams earned an annual salary of $25,000, equivalent to $408,759.12 today (by comparison, George W. Bush's salary in 2006 was $400,000). The yearly rent on the President's House, in Philadelphia, was $2,700 ($44,145.99 today).

Power always thinks . . . that it is doing God's service when it is violating all his laws.

When it is in our Power, without any Difficulty, to raise many other Commodities, enough not only for our own Consumption, but for Exportation, will it be credited without surprize, that we send every Year, allmost the whole Globe over, for such Commodities to import such Commodities for our own Use?

The sources of our Wealth are dried away. And unless we seek for Resources, from Agriculture Improvements in our Agriculture and an Augmentation of our Commerce, we must forego the Pleasure of Delicacies and ornaments, if not the Comfort of real Necessaries, both in Diet and Apparell.

No free man can be separated from his property but by his own act or fault.

—From a letter protesting
the Stamp Act,
1765

From

Dissertation on the Canon and the Feudal Law, in the
Boston Gazette, August 1765.

Property is surely a right of mankind as real as liberty.

◈

*T*he people have a right, an indisputable, un-
alienable, indefeasible, divine right to that most
dreaded and envied kind of knowledge—I mean of the
character and conduct of their rulers.

◈

*T*he jaws of power are always opened to devour,
and her arm is always stretched out, if possible,
to destroy the freedom of thinking, speaking, and writing.

◈

Formalities and Ceremonies are an abomination in my sight. I hate them, in Religion, Government, Science, Life.

—From a diary entry, June 30, 1770

There is danger from all men. The only maxim of a free government ought to be to trust no man living with power to endanger the public liberty.

—From a diary entry, 1772

Nip *the shoots* of arbitrary power in the bud, is the only maxim which can ever preserve the liberties of any people.

—From the **Boston Gazette**, February 6, 1775

We may please ourselves with the prospect of free and popular governments. But there is great danger that those governments will not make us happy.

—In a letter to James Warren, April 16, 1776

*I*s it not equally true, that Men in general in every Society, who are wholly destitute of Property, are also too little acquainted with public Affairs to form a Right Judgment, and too dependent upon other Men to have a Will of their own?

❖

*S*uch is the Frailty of the human Heart, that very few Men, who have no Property, have any Judgment of their own. They talk and vote as they are directed by Some Man of Property, who has attached their Minds to his Interest.

❖

The idea of a man born a magistrate, lawgiver, or judge is absurd and unnatural.

—From *The Constitution of the Commonwealth of Massachusetts*, 1780

All *offices would be monopolized* by the rich; the poor and the middling ranks would be excluded and an aristocratic despotism would immediately follow.

—From a letter to John Jebb, regarding the Pennsylvania Constitution, August 21, 1785

All the perplexities, confusions, and distresses in America arise, not from defects in their constitution or confederation, not from a want of honor or virtue, so much as from downright ignorance of the nature of coin, credit, and circulation.

—FROM A LETTER TO THOMAS JEFFERSON, AUGUST 25, 1787

I have long been settled in my opinion, that neither Philosophy, nor Religion, nor Morality, nor Wisdom, nor Interest, will ever govern nations or Parties against their Vanity, their Pride, their Resentment or Revenge, or their Avarice or Ambition. Nothing but Force and Power and Strength can restrain them.

—From a letter to Thomas Jefferson, October 9, 1787

The moment the idea is admitted into society that property is not as sacred as the law of God, and that there is not a force of law and public justice to protect it, anarchy and tyranny commence.

—From *A Defence of the Constitutions of Government of the United States of America,* 1787

It is weakness rather than wickedness which renders men unfit to be trusted with unlimited power.

—1788

From

Adams's State of the Union Address, November 12, 1797.

*T*he commerce of the United States is essential, if not to their existence, at least to their comfort, their growth, prosperity, and happiness.

◆

*T*he genius, character, and habits of the people are highly commercial. Their cities have been formed and exist upon commerce. Our agriculture, fisheries, arts, and manufactures are connected with and depend upon it. In short, commerce has made this country what it is, and it can not be destroyed or neglected without involving the people in poverty and distress.

◆

I should hold myself guilty of a neglect of duty if I forbore to recommend that we should make every exertion to protect our commerce and to place our country in a suitable posture of defense as the only sure means of preserving both.

◈

S ince the decay of the feudal system, by which the public defense was provided for chiefly at the expense of individuals, the system of loans has been introduced, and as no nation can raise within the year by taxes sufficient sums for its defense and military operations in time of war the sums loaned and debts contracted have necessarily become the subjects of what have been called funding systems. The consequences arising from the continual accumulation of public debts in other countries ought to admonish us to be careful to prevent their growth in our own.

◈

I *pray Heaven to bestow the best blessings* on this house and all that shall hereafter inhabit. May none but honest and wise men ever rule under this roof.

—Referring to the White House in a letter to Abigail, November 2, 1800

I had forgotten the custom of putting Prophets in the Stocks . . . . It may be thought impiety by many, but I could not help wishing that the ancient practice had been continued down to more modern times and that all the Prophets at least from Peter the Hermit, to Nimrod Hews inclusively, had been confined in the Stocks and prevented from spreading so many delusions and shedding so much blood.

—In a letter to Thomas Jefferson, May 3, 1812

As *long as Property exists*, it will accumulate in Individuals and Families. As long as Marriage exists, Knowledge, Property and Influence will accumulate in Families.

—From a letter to Thomas Jefferson,
July 16, 1814

The fundamental article of my *political creed* is that despotism, or unlimited sovereignty, or absolute power, is the same in a majority of a popular assembly, an aristocratical council, an ogliarchical junto, and a single emperor.

—In a letter to Thomas Jefferson, November 13, 1815

You ask, how has it happened that all Europe has acted on the principle, "that Power was Right".... Power always sincerely, conscientiously, *de tres bon foi*, believes itself right.... Power must never be trusted without a check.

—In a letter to Thomas Jefferson, February 2, 1816

Congress assembled and proceeded to Business, and the Members appeared to me to be of one Mind, and that mind after my own heart. I dreaded the danger of disunion and divisions among Us, and much more among the People. It appeared to me, that all Petitions, Remonstrances and Negotiations, for the future would be fruitless and only occasion a Loss of time and give Opportunity to the Ennemy to sow divisions among the States and the People.

—From *The Adams Papers: Diary and Autobiography of John Adams*

Shall we have recourse to the art of printing? But this has not destroyed property or aristocracy or corporations or paper wealth in England or America, or diminished the influence of either; on the contrary, it has multiplied aristocracy and diminished democracy.

—In a letter to John Taylor

How few aim at the good of the whole, without aiming too much at the prosperity of parts!

—In a letter to son-in-law William Smith

My Position was this — that that Gentlemans System would end in the total destruction of American Liberty. I never shall dispute self evident Propositions.

—FROM A DIARY ENTRY

Because power corrupts, society's demands for moral authority and character increase as the importance of the position increases.

In every society where property exists there will ever be a struggle between rich and poor. Mixed in one assembly, equal laws can never be expected; they will either be made by the members to plunder the few who are rich, or by the influence to fleece the many who are poor.

John Adams's nickname, given to him by Thomas Jefferson, was the "Colossus of Independence." He was also called the "Atlas of Independence," and both names were in reference not only to the role he played in the *Declaration of Independence* but also his tireless defense of independence and disdain for those who used power for their own good.

Six

BY PREJUDICES AND PASSIONS: ADAMS ON HIS FELLOW MAN

If John Adams and Thomas Jefferson were alive today, no doubt their Blackberrys would beep constantly with e-mails sent back and forth and back and forth. They couldn't help themselves even back in the days of snail mail! This age of technology would have certainly enabled their addiction to discourse and knowledge.

In 1777, Jefferson wrote to Adams: "Our people, merely for want of intelligence which they may rely on, are become lethargic and insensible of the state they are in." Many years later, after their relationship had turned a bit more competitive, Adams wrote to Jefferson, "You and I ought not to die before we have explained ourselves to each other." Fortunately, they had thirteen more years after he penned this letter, and before each passed away, to explain themselves.

Adams had a way of engaging people by letting him know that he cared about them and their thoughts. He enjoyed agreeing with people, but even more, he liked to debate. In his quest for knowledge and understanding, Adams seemed to be particularly fond of mixing specific issues with general thought. For example, he might discuss the future of the newborn nation while also contemplating human nature. Consideration of his fellow man only increased with age. It was a topic that clearly interested Adams and he found reason to share his views with others, wife Abigail even more than friend Jefferson. In reading his words, it seems that Adams sometimes used his letters to make sense of his observations and to then turn them into cogent thought. The quotes that follow are all arranged around a central theme: one man trying to understand his fellow man and what motivated him, troubled him, and most important, caused him to act unjustly (at times) toward others.

Some of the e-mails to emerge from the Adams Blackberry would be of a more personal nature. He would often comment on his friends and colleagues, assessing their actions and inadvertently leaving a legacy of opinion for historians to make gospel or take with a grain of salt. Either way, history seems to have been kind to Mr. Adams.

Only three presidents did not attend the inaugural cere-
mony of their successor: John Adams, John Quincy Adams,
and Andrew Johnson. Presidential historian Michael Bes-
chloss wrote that Adams was, "so disappointed by his defeat
that he refused to attend his successor's swearing-in." His
successor, Jefferson, was a friend, but he was a Federalist
and a bitter rivalry had formed between the Republicans
and Federalists during the campaign. Fortunately, despite
the hurt feelings and the inaugural snub, the friendship
between Adams and Jefferson survived.

A *Pen* is certainly an *excellent Instrument*, to
fix a Mans Attention and to inflame his Ambition.

—From a diary entry, November 14, 1760

Human Nature is not so stupid or so abandoned, as many worthy men imagine, and even the common People, if their peculiar Customs and Modes of thinking are a little studied, [are not] so ungrateful, or untractible, but that their Labours may be conducted, by the Genius and Experience of a few, to very great and useful Purposes.

—FROM THE *BOSTON GAZETTE*, JULY 18, 1763

Man is distinguished from other animals, his fellow inhabitants of this planet, by a capacity of acquiring knowledge and civility, more than by any excellency, corporeal, or mental, with which mere nature has furnished his species. His erect figure and sublime countenance would give him but little elevation above the bear or the tiger; nay, notwithstanding those advantages, he would hold an inferior rank in the scale of being, and would have a worse prospect of happiness than those creatures, were it not for the capacity of uniting with others, and availing himself of arts and inventions in social life.

—In a published letter, August 1, 1763

Suits generally Spring from Passion. Jones vs. Bigelow, Cotton and Nye arose from Ambition . . . Such Rivals have no Friendship for each other. From such Rivalries originate Quarrells Contentions, Quarrells and Suits. Actions of Defamation are the usual Fruits of such Competitions. What affection can there be between two Rival Candidates for the Confidence of a Town? The famous Action of slander at Worcester between Hopkins and Ward, of Rhode Island, Sprouted from the same Stock. There the Aim was at the Confidence of the Colony.

—From a diary entry, April 4, 1767

It is no Damage to a young Man to learn the Art of living, early, if it is at the Expence of much musing and pondering and Anxiety.

—From a diary entry, June 27, 1770

Facts are stubborn things; and whatever may be our wishes, our inclinations, or the dictates of our passions, they cannot alter the state of facts and evidence.

—From the argument in defense of the soldiers in the Boston Massacre trials, December 1770

There is not in human nature a more wonderful phenomenon, nor in the whole theory of it a more intricate speculation, than the shiftings, turnings, windings, and evasions of a guilty conscience. Such is our unalterable moral constitution, that an internal inclination to do wrong is criminal; and a wicked thought stains the mind with guilt, and makes it tingle with pain. Hence it comes to pass, that the guilty mind can never bear to think that its guilt is known to God or man, no, nor to itself.

—FROM *NOVANGLUS*, FEBRUARY 13, 1775

The human mind is not naturally the clearest atmosphere; but the clouds and vapors which have been raised in it by the artifices of temporal and spiritual tyrants, have made it impossible to see objects in it distinctly.

—From *Novanglus*, March 6, 1775

All sober inquirers after truth, ancient and modern, pagan and Christian, have declared that the happiness of man, as well as his dignity, consists in virtue. Confucius, Zoroaster, Socrates, Mahomet, not to mention authorities really sacred, have agreed in this.

—From *Thoughts on Government*, 1776

Resentment is a Passion, implanted by Nature for the Preservation of the Individual. Injury is the Object which excites it.

—From a diary entry, March 4, 1776

All *great changes are irksome* to the human mind, especially those which are attended with great dangers and uncertain effects. No man living can foresee the consequences of such a measure.

—In a letter to James Warren, regarding fears over the impending revolution, April 22, 1776

Injustice, Wrong, Injury excites the Feeling of Resentment, as naturally and necessarily as Frost and Ice excite the feeling of cold, as fire excites heat, and as both excite Pain. A Man may have the Faculty of concealing his Resentment, or suppressing it, but he must and ought to feel it. Nay he ought to indulge it, to cultivate it. It is a Duty. His Person, his Property, his Liberty, his Reputation are not safe without it. He ought, for his own Security and Honour, and for the public good to punish those who injure him, unless they repent, and then he should forgive, having Satisfaction and Compensation. Revenge is unlawfull. It is the same with Communities. They ought to resent and to punish.

—From a diary entry, March 4, 1776

Some people must have time to look around them, before, behind, on the right hand, and on the left, and then to think, and after all this to resolve. Others see at one intuitive glance into the past and the future, and judge with precision at once. But remember you can't make thirteen clocks strike precisely alike at the same second.

—Describing the debates over declaring independence
in the Continental Congress, 1776

I believe there is no one principle which predominates in human nature so much in every stage of life, from the cradle to the grave, in males and females, old and young, black and white, rich and poor, high and low, as this passion for superiority.

—From a letter to Abigail, May 22, 1777

The Practice of profane Cursing and Swearing, so silly as well as detestable, prevails in a most abominable Degree. It is indulged and connived at by Officers, and practised too in such a Manner that there is no Kind of Check against it. And I take upon me to say that order of every Kind will be lax as long as this is so much the Case.

—From a diary entry, February 26, 1778

Virtue is not always amiable.
Integrity is sometimes ruined by Prejudices and by Passions.

—From a diary entry, February 9, 1779

In Travelling the best Way is to dine and sup at the Taverns, with the Company, avec les autres as they express it. You meet here, a vast Variety of Company, which is decent, and after a few Coups du Vin, their Tongues run very fast and you learn more of the Language, the Manners, the Customs, Laws, Politicks, Arts, &c. in this Way, perhaps than in any other. You should preserve your Dignity, talk little, listen much, not be very familiar with any in particular, for there are Sharpers, Gamblers, Quack Doctors, Strolling Comediens, in short People of all Characters, assembled at these Dinners and Suppers, and without Caution, you may be taken into Parties of Pleasure and Diversion that will cost you very dear.

—From a diary entry, written in France, April 22, 1779

The Difference between the Faces and Airs of the French and Spanish Officers, is more obvious and striking than that of their Uniforms. Gravity and Silence distinguish the one, Gaiety and Vivacity and Loquacity the others.

—From a diary entry, December 9, 1779

Edgehill and Worcester were curious and interesting to us, as Scaenes where Freemen had fought for their Rights. The People in the Neighbourhood, appeared so ignorant and careless at Worcester that I was provoked and asked, "And do Englishmen so soon forget the Ground where Liberty was fought for? Tell your Neighbours and your Children that this is holy Ground, much holier than that on which your Churches stand. All England should come in Pilgrimage to this Hill, once a Year." This animated them, and they seemed much pleased with it. Perhaps their Aukwardness before might arise from their Uncertainty of our Sentiments concerning the Civil Wars.

—From a diary entry about a tour of the English countryside,
taken with Thomas Jefferson, April 4-10, 1786

I find men and manners, principles and opinions, much altered in this country since I left it.
—Despairing about political greed,
to his daughter Nabby, 1788

When one family is depressed, either in a monarchy or in any species of republic, another must arise.

—From **Discourse on Davila**, 1790

A desire to be observed, considered, esteemed, praised, beloved, and admired by his fellows is one of the earliest as well as the keenest dispositions discovered in the heart of man.

—From Discourse on Davila, 1790

I *could express my Faith* in shorter terms. He who loves the Workman and his Work, and does what he can to preserve and improve it, shall be accepted of him.

—In a letter to Thomas Jefferson,
June 18, 1812

If human Life is a Bubble, no matter how soon it breaks. If it is as I firmly believe an immortal Existence We ought patiently to wait the Instructions of the great Teacher. I am, Sir, your deeply afflicted Friend.

—IN A LETTER TO THOMAS JEFFERSON, OCTOBER 20, 1815

I believe there is no individual totally
depraved. The most abandoned scoundrel that ever existed,
never yet Wholly extinguished his Conscience, and while
Conscience remains there is some religion.

—From a letter to Thomas Jefferson, 1817

Integrity should be preserved in all events, as
essential to his happiness, through every stage of
his existence. His first maxim then should be to
place his honor out of reach of all men.

—In a letter to Thomas, his son

Adams on

the excessive use of force, the need for a strong judicial branch, and the dangers of self-deceit.

*W*restling, running, leaping, lifting, and other exercises of strength, hardiness, courage, and activity, may be promoted among private soldiers, common sailors, laborers, manufacturers, and husbandmen, among whom they are most wanted, provided sufficient precautions are taken that no romantic, cavalier-like principles of honor intermix with them, and render a resignation of the right of judging, and the power of executing, to the public, shameful.

◈

A certain set of sentiments have been lately so fashionable, that you could go into few companies without hearing such smart sayings as these, If a man should insult me, by kicking my shins, and I had a sword by my side I would make the sun shine through him; if any man, let him be as big as Goliath, should take me by the nose, I would let his bowels out with my sword, if I had one, and if I had none, I would beat his brains out with the first club I could find . . .

◆

But whenever such notions spread so inimical to the peace of society, that boxing, clubs, swords, or firearms, are resorted to for deciding every quarrel, about a girl, a game at cards, or any little accident that wine or folly or jealousy may suspect to be an affront, the whole power of the government should be exerted to suppress them.

◆

There is nothing in the science of human nature more curious, or that deserves a critical attention from every order of men so much, as that principle which moral writers have distinguished by the name of self-deceit. This principle is the spurious offspring of self-love; and is, perhaps, the source of far the greatest and worst part of the vices and calamities among mankind.

◆

It's simply a matter of doing what you do best and not worrying about what the other fellow is going to do.

Happiness, whether in despotism or democracy, whether in slavery or liberty, can never be found without virtue.

Grief drives men to serious reflection, sharpens the understanding and softens the heart.

Did you ever see a portrait of a great man without perceiving strong traits of pain and anxiety?

There are two educations. One should teach us how to make a living and the other how to live.

Adams's observations
of fellow founding father Benjamin Franklin.

He had wit at will.

◆

*H*e had talents of irony, allegory, and fable that he could adapt with great skill to the promotion of moral and political truth.

◆

*H*is masterly acquaintance with the French language, his extensive correspondence in France, his great addresses, united to his unshaken firmness in the present American system of politics and war, point him out as the fittest character for this momentous undertaking.

—Describing Franklin as an ambassador to France, 1776

From Adams's Senate address,
following the death of George Washington.

*T*he life of our Washington can not suffer by comparison with those of other countries who have been most celebrated and exalted by fame. The attributes and decorations of royalty could have only served to eclipse the majesty of those virtues which made him, from being a modest citizen, a more resplendent luminary.

◆

*H*is example is now complete, and it will teach wisdom and virtue to magistrates, citizens, and men, not only in the present age, but in future generations as long as our history shall be read.

◆

On

Adams's friend and sometimes rival, Thomas Jefferson.

*J*efferson thinks he shall by this step get a reputation of a humble modest, meek man, wholly without ambition or vanity. He may even have deceived himself into this belief.

—After Jefferson resigned as Secretary of State, 1793

❖

*M*r. Jefferson has reason to reflect upon himself. How he will get rid of his remorse in his retirement, I know not. He must know that he leaves the government infinitely worse than he found it, and that from his own error or ignorance.

—From a letter to Benjamin Rush, April 18, 1808

❖

The Manners of Maryland are somewhat peculiar. They have but few Merchants. They are chiefly Planters and Farmers. The Planters are those who raise Tobacco and the Farmers such as raise Wheat &c. The Lands are cultivated, and all Sorts of Trades are exercised by Negroes, or by transported Convicts, which has occasioned the Planters and Farmers to assume the Title of Gentlemen, and they hold their Negroes and Convicts, that is all labouring People and Tradesmen, in such Contempt, that they think themselves a distinct order of Beings. Hence they never will suffer their Sons to labour or learn any Trade, but they bring them up in Idleness or what is worse in Horse Racing, Cock fighting, and Card Playing.

—From a diary entry, February 23, 1777

Great Numbers emigrate to the back parts of North and S.C. [South Carolina] and G.[Georgia] for the Sake of living without Trouble. The Woods, such is the mildness of the Climate, produce grass to support horses and Cattle, and Chesnuts, Acorns and other Things for the food of hogs. So that they have only a little corn to raise which is done without much Labour. They call this kind of Life following the range. They are very ignorant and hate all Men of Education. They call them Pen and Ink Men.

—From a diary entry, November 1791

In all Countries, and in all Companies for several Years, I have in Conversation and in Writing, enumerated The Towns, Militia, Schools and Churches as the four Causes of the Grouth and Defence of N. England. The Virtues and Talents of the People are there formed. Their Temperance, Patience, Fortitude, Prudence, and justice, as well as their Sagacity, Knowledge, Judgment, Taste, Skill, Ingenuity, Dexterity, and Industry.

—From a diary entry, written in London

When Thomas Jefferson defeated John Adams in the election of 1800, it was the first and only time that a president ran against his vice president. Needless to say, Adams was not pleased to lose to his VP, even if Jefferson was a friend.

Seven

FOOLISH TRUMPERY:
ADAMS ON RELIGION

John Adams might not have grown up to be a man of the cloth, as his father wished, but he did marry the daughter of the town's minister. And as his writing and conversations prove, religion was something that Adams gave great thought to throughout his life.

Adams was a political philosopher by nature, but always with an eye on history. And when critiquing the world's religions, he did so from a historical perspective. Adams believed that religion had a place in America, and even in American politics, but was very disappointed in the violence and upset that had resulted from religious fervor around the world. As with conflict, he believed that religious matters should be handled with great prudence.

Lemuel Briant, the minister at Adams's church (First Parish, in Braintree), had a tremendous influence on the future president. In particular, Briant believed in the role of free will, and this fed Adams's faith in the capabilities of the human mind. Briant also questioned the ideas of original sin, and such opinions made him the target of public scorn. However, Adams and his father appreciated the dialogue brought on by such thought-provoking questions. Briant was so controversial that he was nearly run out of town until the elder Adams stepped up to defend him. It's no wonder John Adams didn't hesitate to share controversial opinions of his own, and it's no wonder he decided against a life in the ministry.

Another minister, Jonathan Mayhew, spoke at length about civil liberties and freedom of thought and this influenced Adams's idea of an ideal government. He did not believe in predestination, so it makes sense that he'd be willing to lend his support to a declaration of independence from a king. Whereas others thought it their fate to be colonized, Adams saw a chance to use his God-given abilities to make his own fate.

In a letter to Benjamin Rush, Adams summarized his respect for religion while also sprinkling in some of the cynicism that was present in much of his writing: "I have attended public worship in all countries and with all sects and believe them all much better than no religion, though I have not thought myself obliged to believe all I heard." And that, in a nutshell, is John Adams on religion.

John Adams is buried in a crypt beneath the United First Parish Church in Quincy, Massachusetts. The church was built with money that he donated.

The frightful engines of *ecclesiastical councils*, of diabolical malice, and Calvinistical good-nature never failed to terrify me exceedingly whenever I thought of preaching.

—In a letter to Richard Cranch explaining why he chose not to be a minister, October 18, 1756

I found that County *hot with controversy.* Mr. Maccarty though a Calvinist was not a bigot, but the Town was the scene of disputes all the time I lived there.

—Writing of Thaddeus Maccarty, who gave Adams his first teaching job, and the town of Worcester

Dissertation on the Canon and the Feudal Law, which appeared in the *Boston Gazette*, August 1765.

*L*et the pulpit resound with the doctrines and sentiments of religious liberty. Let us hear the dangers of thralldom to our consciences from ignorance, extreme poverty, and dependence; in short, from civil and political slavery. Let us see delineated before us the true map of man.

◈

*L*et us hear the dignity of his nature, and the noble rank he holds among the works of God—that consenting to slavery is a sacrilegious breach of trust, as offensive in the sight of God as it is derogatory from our own honor or interest or happiness—and that God Almighty has promulgated from heaven liberty, peace, and goodwill to man!

*N*umberless have been the systems of iniquity The most refined, sublime, extensive, and astonishing constitution of policy that ever was conceived by the mind of man was framed by the Romish clergy for the aggrandizement of their own Order They even persuaded mankind to believe, faithfully and undoubtingly, that God Almighty had entrusted them with the keys of heaven . . .

◈

*A*ll these opinions they were enabled to spread and rivet among the people by reducing their minds to a state of sordid ignorance and staring timidity, and by infusing into them a religious horror of letters and knowledge. Thus was human nature chained fast for ages in a cruel, shameful, and deplorable servitude to him and his subordinate tyrants, who, it was foretold, would exalt himself above all that was called God and that was worshipped.

◈

*O*f all the nonsense and delusion which had ever passed through the mind of man, none had ever been more extravagant than the notions of absolutions, indelible characters, uninterrupted successions, and the rest of those fantastical ideas, derived from the canon law, which had thrown such a glare of mystery, sanctity, reverence, and right reverend eminence and holiness around the idea of a priest as no mortal could deserve.

◈

It is the duty of the clergy to accommodate their discourses to the times, to preach against such sins as are most prevalent, and recommend such virtues as are most wanted. For example, if exorbitant ambition and venality are predominant, ought they not to warn their hearers against those vices? If public spirit is much wanted, should they not inculcate this great virtue? If the rights and duties of Christian magistrates and subjects are disputed, should they not explain them, show their nature, ends, limitations, and restrictions, how muchsoever it may move the gall of Massachusetts.

—In the *Boston Gazette*, 1774

Although the detail of the formation of the American governments is at present little known or regarded either in Europe or in America, it may hereafter become an object of curiosity. It will never be pretended that any persons employed in that service had interviews with the gods, or were in any degree under the influence of Heaven, more than those at work upon ships or houses, or laboring in merchandise or agriculture; it will forever be acknowledged that these governments were contrived merely by the use of reason and the senses.

—From *A Defence of the Constitutions of Government of the United States of America*, 1787

It is to me a most affecting thing to hear myself prayed for, in particular as I do every day in a week, and disposes me to bear with more composure, some disagreeable circumstances that attend my situation.

—From a letter to Abigail, 1789

The Christian Religion is, above all the Religions that ever prevailed or existed in ancient or modern Times, The Religion of Wisdom, Virtue, Equity and Humanity, let the Blackguard Paine say what he will. It is Resignation to God—it is Goodness itself to Man.

—From a diary entry, July 26, 1796

One great Advantage of the Christian Religion is that it brings the great Principle of the Law of Nature and Nations, Love your Neighbour as yourself, and do to others as you would that others should do to you, to the Knowledge, Belief and Veneration of the whole People.

—From a diary entry, August 14, 1796

Children, Servants, Women and Men are all Professors in the science of public as well as private Morality. No other Institution for Education, no kind of political Discipline, could diffuse this kind of necessary Information, so universally among all Ranks and Descriptions of Citizens.

—Describing the Christian religion in a diary entry,
August 14, 1796

I will insist that the Hebrews have done more to civilize men than any other nation. If I were an atheist, and believed in blind eternal fate, I should still believe that fate had ordained the Jews to be the most essential instrument for civilizing the nations.

— IN A LETTER TO F. A. VANDERKEMP, FEBRUARY 16, 1809

Religion and *virtue* are the only foundations, not of republicanism and of all free government, but of social felicity under all government and in all the combinations of human society.

—FROM A LETTER TO BENJAMIN RUSH, 1811

From letters

Adams wrote to John Taylor.

*T*he priesthood have, in all ancient nations, nearly monopolized learning.... And, even since the Reformation, when or where has existed a Protestant or dissenting sect who would tolerate A FREE INQUIRY?

—1814

*T*he blackest billingsgate, the most ungentlemanly insolence, the most yahooish brutality is patiently endured, countenanced, propagated, and applauded. But touch a solemn truth in collision with a dogma of a sect, though capable of the clearest proof, and you will soon find you have disturbed a nest, and the hornets will swarm about your legs and hands, and fly into your face and eyes.

—1814

What havoc has been made of books through every century of the Christian era? Where are fifty gospels, condemned as spurious by the bull of Pope Gelasius? Where are the forty wagon-loads of Hebrew manuscripts burned in France, by order of another pope, because suspected of heresy? Remember the index expurgatorius, the inquisition, the stake, the axe, the halter, and the guillotine.

—1814

◆

Have you considered that system of holy lies and pious frauds that has raged and triumphed for 1,500 years.

—1814

◆

As I *understand the Christian religion*, it was, and is, a revelation. But how has it happened that millions of fables, tales, legends, have been blended with both Jewish and Christian revelation that have made them the most bloody religion that ever existed?

—In a letter to FA Van der Kamp, December 27, 1816

This oration will be read five hundred years hence with as much rapture as it was heard. It ought to be read at the end of every century, and indeed at the end of every year, forever and ever.

—Discussing the quote "Whatever makes men good Christians, makes them good citizens" in a speech at Plymouth, December 22, 1820

The most afflictive circumstances that I have witnessed in the lot of humanity are the narrow views, the unsocial humour, the fastidious scorn and repulsive tempers of all denominations excepting one.

—Writing to Aaron Bancroft,
in support of the Unitarianism, in 1823

The Church of Rome has made it an article of faith that no man can be saved out of their church, and all other religious sects approach this dreadful opinion in proportion to their ignorance, and the influence of ignorant or wicked priests.

—From *The Adams Papers: Diary and Autobiography of John Adams*

Words shared with

Thomas Jefferson in letters.

God has infinite Wisdom, goodness and power. He created the Universe. His duration is eternal ....His presence is as extensive as Space. What is Space? an infinite, spherical Vacuum. He created this Speck of Dirt and the human Species for his glory: and with the deliberate design of making nine tenths of our Species miserable forever, for his glory. This is the doctrine of Christian Theologians in general: ten to one.

—SEPTEMBER 14, 1813

Indeed, Mr. Jefferson, what could be invented to debase the ancient Christianism which Greeks, Romans, Hebrews and Christian factions, above all the Catholics, have not fraudulently imposed upon the public? Miracles after miracles have rolled down in torrents.

—FROM A LETTER TO THOMAS JEFFERSON, DECEMBER 3, 1813

Cabalistic Christianity, which is Catholic Christianity, and which has prevailed for 1,500 years, has received a mortal wound, of which the monster must finally die. Yet so strong is his constitution, that he may endure for centuries before he expires.

—IN A LETTER TO THOMAS JEFFERSON, JULY 16, 1814

The question before the human race is, whether the God of nature shall govern the world by his own laws, or whether priests and kings shall rule it by fictitious miracles?

—JOHN ADAMS IN A LETTER TO THOMAS JEFFERSON, JUNE 20, 1815

I do not like the reappearance of the Jesuits…. Shall we not have regular swarms of them here, in as many disguises as only a king of the gipsies can assume, dressed as printers, publishers, writers and schoolmasters? If ever there was a body of men who merited damnation on earth and in Hell, it is this society of Loyola's. Nevertheless, we are compelled by our system of religious toleration to offer them an asylum.

—MAY 5, 1816

My history of the Jesuits is not elegantly written, but is supported by unquestionable authorities, is very particular and very horrible. Their restoration is indeed "a step toward darkness," cruelty, perfidy, despotism, death and I wish we were out of danger of bigotry and Jesuitism.

—AUGUST 9, 1816

We have now, it Seems a National Bible Society, to propagate King James's Bible, through all Nations. Would it not be better to apply these pious SubScriptions, to purify Christendom from the Corruptions of Christianity; than to propagate those Corruptions in Europe Asia, Africa and America!

—NOVEMBER 4, 1816

My History of the Jesuits is in four volumes.... This society has been a greater calamity to mankind than the French Revolution, or Napoleon's despotism or ideology. It has obstructed progress of reformation and the improvement of the human mind in society much longer and more fatally.

—NOVEMBER 4, 1816

Conclude not from all this that I have renounced the Christian religion. . . . Far from it. I see in every page something to recommend Christianity in its purity, and something to discredit its corruptions. . . . The ten commandments and the sermon on the mount contain my religion.   —NOVEMBER 4, 1816

Twenty times in the course of my late reading have I been on the point of breaking out, "This would be the best of all possible worlds, if there were no religion in it!!!" But in this exclamation I would have been as fanatical as Bryant or Cleverly.
                                        —APRIL 19, 1817

Without religion this world would be something not fit to be mentioned in polite company, I mean Hell.   —APRIL 19, 1817

Oh! Lord! Do you think a Protestant Popedom is annihilated in America? Do you recollect, or have you ever attended to the ecclesiastical Strifes in Maryland Pennsilvania, New York, and every part of New England? What a mercy it is that these People cannot whip and crop, and pillory and roast, as yet in the U.S.! If they could they would. —MAY 18, 1817

God is an essence that we know nothing of. Until this awful blasphemy is got rid of, there never will be any liberal science in the world. —1820

Can a free government possibly exist with the Roman Catholic religion? —MAY 19, 1821

The substance and essence of Christianity, as I understand it, is eternal and unchangeable, and will bear examination forever, but it has been mixed with extraneous ingredients, which I think will not bear examination, and they ought to be separated. Adieu.

—JANUARY 23, 1825

Now, what free inquiry, when a writer must surely encounter the risk of fine or imprisonment for adducing any argument for investigating into the divine authority of those books?

—JANUARY 23, 1825

The divinity of Jesus is made a convenient cover for absurdity. Nowhere in the Gospels do we find a precept for Creeds, Confessions, Oaths, Doctrines, and whole carloads of other foolish trumpery that we find in Christianity.

I almost shudder at the thought of alluding to the most fatal example of the abuses of grief which the history of mankind has preserved-the Cross. Consider what calamities that engine of grief has produced!

I wish You could live a Year in Boston, hear their Divines, read their publications, especially the Repository. You would see how spiritual Tyranny and ecclesiastical Domination are beginning in our Country: at least struggling for birth.

My Adoration of the Author of the Universe is too profound and too sincere.

John Adams was a Unitarian. Unitarianism was a liberal religious movement based on rationalism and it unified a number of non-conforming Protestant sects. At the heart of Unitarianism was the idea that religious opinions are completely up to the individual. Joseph Priestly (the scientist who discovered carbon dioxide and photosynthesis) and John Stuart Mill (the most influential philosopher of the nineteenth century) were also Unitarians.

Eight

DONE WITH REFLECTION:
ADAMS AS PHILOSOPHER
AND FUNNY GUY

In addition to Joseph Priestly, Adams read a lot of Johann Wolfgang von Goethe, who was a believer in humans reaching their full potential. Adams was also fond of John Locke, who stated that knowledge grew out of reflection and that ideas grew out of experiences. Locke's *Two Treatises of Government* argued against divine right and absolute monarchy, which appealed to Adams, as did Locke's belief that through a "social contract" political order could be maintained without infringing on individual rights. David Hume was another Adams favorite—he appreciated Hume's faith in the human mind and his skeptical views of religion and Great Britain's royal society. If alive today, one could argue that Adams would also subscribe to the philosophies of Will Ferrell and Steve Carell. No doubt, he would be a regular viewer, and probable guest, of Jon Stewart and Stephen Colbert. He was a funny guy, after all.

A reading of the works of John Adams reveals a man with an appreciable sense of humor. His ninety years were full of excitement and danger, but also several funny situations. One story goes that when Adams arrived in France as ambassador, he got a kick out of the greeting he received from the French people. They called him "le fameux Adams," mistaking him for his cousin Samuel. They also gave him credit for penning *Common Sense*, an irony considering how much he despised Paine's pamphlet. Another tale finds Adams stopping at an inn one night and sitting down by the fire for a drink and some conversation. The farmers there, much to his happiness, are patriots. And much to his delight is the fact that they speak to Adams, about Adams, without ever realizing that he is Adams. And finally, while on the road in the winter of 1776, Benjamin Franklin and Adams had to share a room with just one bed. That was no problem, but like an old married couple the two argued over the window and whether it should stay open! Franklin welcomed the chilly conditions, believing it was healthy to sleep with fresh air. Adams disliked the cold and wanted to be snug and warm. There must have been a funny quote or two uttered that night, but none was recorded. Perhaps this is best.

Adams was able to combine hyperbole with introspection. He was being honest when he questioned the importance of his job as vice president and when describing what would have become of him had he defeated Jefferson in 1800. He could even joke about the *Declaration of Independence*, Congress, and the way history would portray George

Washington and Benjamin Franklin. Funny stuff from a funny founding father.

Good humor aside, most of his observations were philosophical in nature. In 1755, he published his *Novanglus* essay which questioned Parliament's right to regulate the colonies with laws the colonists did not want and taxes they hadn't agreed to pay. Ten years later, he published his *Dissertation on the Canon and Feudal Law*, which managed to touch on philosophy and religion while also blasting away with both barrels at the recently levied Stamp Tax. In *Dissertation*, Adams credited the settlement of the New World to God, but also to ideas of enlightenment and freedom. In the fight for liberty, he saw a fight against tyranny. Adams wrote that government must respect "the dignity of human nature." This phrase would become a patriotic rally cry. In his 1777 work *Thoughts on Government*, Adams mapped out a government that could meet the needs of the people, outlining a system that included a judicial branch, bicameral legislative branch, and an executive branch. One decade later his *Defense of the Constitutions of Government of the United States of America* made a passionate case for self-determination.

"Reason holds the helm, but passions are the gale," Adams wrote. There's the philosophical side. "Thanks to God that he gave me stubbornness when I know I am right." And that would be the funny side!

On April 24, 1800, under Adams's guidance, Congress approved $5,900 for the purchase of books for a Library of Congress ($5,900 is roughly the equivalent of $100,000 today). The books—740 volumes and three maps—were ordered from London and arrived in Washington, D.C. in 1801.

Let us tenderly and kindly cherish, therefore, the means of knowledge. Let us dare to read, think, speak, and write.

—In *Dissertation on the Canon and Feudal Law,*
from the Boston Gazette, August 1765

Author of our religion has taught us that trivial provocations are to be overlooked; and that if a man should offer you an insult, by boxing one ear, rather than indulge a furious passion and return blow for blow, you ought even to turn the other also. This expression, however, though it inculcates strongly the duty of moderation and self-government upon sudden provocations, imports nothing against the right of resistance or of self-defence.

—In a published letter, September 5, 1768

The reason is, because it's of more importance to community, that innocence should be protected, than it is, that guilt should be punished.

—From the argument in defense of the soldiers in the Boston Massacre trials, December 1770

Fear is the foundation of most governments, but it is so sordid and brutal a passion, and renders men in whose breasts it predominates so stupid and miserable, that Americans will not be likely to approve of any political institution which is founded on it.

—FROM *THOUGHTS ON GOVERNMENT*, 1776

*The happiness of society
is the end of government.*

—From *Thoughts on Government*, 1776

You will never be alone
with a poet in your pocket.

—From a letter to John Quincy,
May 14, 1781

I hold the concealment of sentiments to be no better than countenancing sedition.

—From a conversation with
Benjamin Franklin, 1787

I am reading a Work of Cicero that I remember not to have read before. It is intituled M. Tullii Ciceronis Si Deo placet Consolatio. Remarkable for an ardent hope and confident belief of a future State.

—From a diary entry, August 7, 1796

I *never understood* what a republican government was and I believe no other man ever did or ever will.

—In a letter to Mercy Warren,
July 20, 1807

While all other sciences have advanced, that of government is at a standstill—little better understood, little better practiced now than three or four thousand years ago.

—From a letter to Thomas Jefferson, July 8, 1813

Everything in life
should be done with reflection.

—In a conversation with John Quincy

Man, as man, becomes an object of respect.

—Commenting on the ideas of the Enlightenment

Vain ambition and other vicious motives were charged by the sacred congregation upon Galileo, as the causes of his hypothesis concerning the motion of the earth, and charged so often and with so many terms, as to render the old man at last suspicious, if not satisfied, that the charge was true, though he had been led to this hypothesis by the light of a great genius and deep researches into astronomy.

—In a published letter

Liberty, according to my metaphysics is a self-determining power in an intellectual agent. It implies thought and choice and power.

When *philosophic reason* is clear and certain by intuition or necessary induction, no subsequent revelation supported by prophecies or miracles can supersede it.

Plato taught that revenge was unlawful, although he allowed of self-defence. The divine Courage and perseverance have a magical talisman, before which difficulties disappear and obstacles vanish into air.

I believe if it was moved and seconded that we should come to a resolution that three and two make five, we should be entertained with logic and rhetoric, law, history, politics, and mathematics concerning the subject for two whole days, and then we should pass the resolution unanimously in the affirmative.

—From a letter to Abigail, humorously describing
the tedious debates of the first Continental Congress,
1774

The *Gentlemen* from Pensilvania and Maryland, complain of the growing Practice of distilling Wheat into Whisky. They say it will become a Question whether the People shall eat bread or drink Whisky.

—From a diary entry, February 6, 1777

The longer I live and the more I see of public men, the more I wish to be a private one. Modesty is a virtue that can never thrive in public.

—1778

The history of our Revolution will be one continued lie from one end to the other. The essence of the whole will be that Dr. Franklin's electrical rod smote the earth and out sprang General Washington. That Franklin electrified him with his rod—and thenceforward these two conducted all the policies, negotiations, legislatures, and war.

—From a letter to Benjamin Rush, 1790

I laugh at myself twenty times a day, for my feelings, and [the] meditations and speculations in which I find myself engaged: Vanity suffers. Cold feelings of unpopularity. Humble reflections.

—FROM A DIARY ENTRY DESCRIBING THE STRESS OF POSSIBLY
BECOMING PRESIDENT, DECEMBER 7, 1796

I have accepted a seat in the House of Representatives, and thereby have consented to my own ruin, to your ruin, and to the ruin of our children. I give you this warning that you may prepare your mind for your fate.

—From a letter to Benjamin Rush, April 12, 1809

Had I been chosen President again, I am certain I could not have lived another year.

—1810 (TEN YEARS AFTER LOSING THE ELECTION
TO THOMAS JEFFERSON)

An Event of the most trifling nature

in Appearance, and fit only to excite Laughter, in other Times, struck me with into a profound Reverie, if not a fit of Melancholly. I met a Man who had sometimes been my Client, and sometimes I had been against him. He, though a common Horse jockey, was sometimes in the right, and I had commonly been successfull in his favour in our Courts of Law. He was always in the Law, and had been sued in many Actions, at almost every Court. As soon as he saw me, he came up to me, and his first Salutation to me was "Oh! Mr. Adams what great Things have you and your Colleagues done for Us! We can never be gratefull enough to you. There are no Courts of Justice now in this Province, and I hope there never will be another!" . . . Is this the Object for which I have been contending? said I to myself, for I rode along without any Answer to this Wretch.

—*From* The Adams Papers: Diary and
Autobiography of John Adams

If there was nothing beyond mortal life, you might be ashamed of your Maker, and compare him to a little Girl amusing herself, her Brothers and Sisters by blowing Bubbles in Soap Sudds.

—In a letter to Thomas Jefferson, concerning
their shared belief in the afterlife

The Declaration of Independence I always considered as a theatrical show. Jefferson ran away with all the stage effect of that… and all the glory of it.

—From a letter to Benjamin Rush,
June 21, 1811

My country has in its wisdom contrived for me the most insignificant office that ever the invention of man contrived or his imagination conceived.

—From a letter to Abigail, regarding his role as vice president

[As president] I refused to suffer in silence. I sighed, sobbed, and groaned, and sometimes screeched and screamed. And I must confess to my shame and sorrow that I sometimes swore.

Every man in [Congress] is a *great man*, an orator, a critic, a statesman; and therefore every man upon every question must show his oratory, his criticism, and his political abilities.

In my many years *I have come to a conclusion* that one useless man is a shame, two is a law firm, and three or more is a congress.

Never trouble trouble till trouble troubles you.

Old minds are like old horses; you must exercise them if you wish to keep them in working order.

> John Adams named his horse Cleopatra. She was his favorite pet and, because of this affection, Adams will always be remembered as the man who ordered the construction of the White House stables. And for being the president who named his horse Cleopatra.

Nine

ALL MY HOPES:
ADAMS AS A FAMILY MAN

In 1764, John Adams and Abigail Smith were married in Weymouth, Massachusetts. John was almost thirty, Abigail not yet twenty. They brought into the world Elizabeth, who died at birth, Susanna, who died in infancy, Charles, who passed away before turning thirty, Abigail, who went by the nickname "Nabby," future president John Quincy, and another son, Thomas. Braintree, Massachusetts was home and it was the only place, according to a lifetime's worth of writing, where he wanted to be. In turn, Abigail was the only woman he wanted to be with, and much has been made of their correspondence.

Adams often sought Abigail's advice and she was more than willing to give it. An early feminist, one of her admonitions was that the government must avoid making the mistake of leaving women out of the political equation. Wisely, Adams promised he'd do his best. Many of Abigail's quotes are included here as they shed light on a side of the second president that most people did not know. It is also interesting to consider the sacrifices he made from the perspective of a dedicated, patriotic wife who was making those sacrifices right alongside him. The stress of separation permeated many of their letters as the nation entered an uncertain war and as Adams tried to serve his fragile country abroad. Abigail was literally an eyewitness to history.

It would be hard to find another childhood that compares to that of John Quincy Adams. As a boy he stood with his mother to watch the Battle of Bunker Hill, and he was old enough and astute enough to be aware of the proceedings of the first and second Continental Congress: such are the benefits—and stresses—that came with being the son of John Adams. But Adams recognized early on what a smart child John Quincy was, and he brought him to Europe during his years as an ambassador there. John Quincy eventually graduated Harvard, became a lawyer, and then, in 1824, was elected the sixth president of the United States. What might be surprising is the fact that he played an important role, as James Monroe's secretary of state, in the formation of the Monroe Doctrine. By offering the protection of the United States to our neighbors in the western hemisphere and by warning European nations what would befall them if they interceded, John Quincy demonstrated that he, too, had a paternal instinct when it came to international affairs. Also in accordance with his father's fierce gestures of independence and intellect, at his inauguration John Quincy was sworn in on a stack of law books instead of a Bible. And like his father, John Quincy argued against slavery, especially later in life when he successfully defended the slaves of the *Amistad*, who had revolted against their captors and did not wish to be returned to the custody of the Spanish in Cuba. He was a man of great conviction who once said, "Always vote for principle, though you may vote alone, and you may cherish the sweetest reflection that your vote is never lost."

In a sadder tale, a laughable incident at Harvard proved prophetic for Charles Adams. Much to his parents' chagrin, Charles was caught streaking, and it was found that alcohol was involved. What might have been a mere college prank proved to be a dependency problem and one that would lead to his early death. Before passing away, he made a bad investment with John Quincy's money and angered his father enough that in 1798 Adams vowed never to see his son again. In the last two years of Charles's life, this proved to be the case.

The youngest son, Thomas, also attended Harvard. Unfortunately, his life resembled more closely that of Charles than John Quincy. He returned home to Braintree, now called Quincy, after his law practice failed and ended up a caretaker of the family farm. He also looked out for Adams after Abigail's death, but alcohol made him an unpleasant companion.

The oldest child, Nabby, was born nine months after her parents' wedding. She married Colonel William Smith and was a close companion of Abigail's during her father's long absences. In the end, her husband got tied up in shady business dealings with her brother Charles, and Nabby died of breast cancer at the age of forty-eight.

It is also worth mentioning that cousin Samuel was more famous, early on, than John, having been a leading figure at the epicenter of the young revolution in Boston. He spoke out against the Stamp Act and was a part of the Boston Tea Party. Over the years, John reached far greater heights, but in fairness this was due to Sam being significantly older than John. There is also the idea of all that John sacrificed by spending so much time abroad and away from his children. Life might have been as good for Thomas and Charles as it was for John Quincy had their father been home more to participate in their upbringing. Generations of Americans may have benefited from Adams's efforts, but nothing comes without a cost.

In 1735, John Adams was born only 75 feet away from the birthplace of his son, John Quincy Adams. It was in this house, called The Old House, that John and Abigail raised their family. John had his law office in the house and it was here that John, Samuel Adams, and James Bowdoin wrote the Massachusetts Constitution. The Stone Library was built next to the house and was fireproof, as per John Quincy's will. The Stone Library is home to over 14,000 volumes and is a part of the Adams National Historic Park in Quincy, Massachusetts.

My Father by his Industry and Enterprize soon became a Person of more Property and Consideration in the Town than his Patron ever was had been. He became a Select Man, a Militia Officer and a Deacon in the Church. He was the honestest Man I ever knew. In Wisdom, Piety, Benevolence and Charity In proportion to his Education and Sphere of Life, I have never seen his Superiour.

—From *The Adams Papers: Diary and Autobiography of John Adams*

For my Children . . . I commit these Memoirs to writing.

—From *The Adams Papers: Diary and Autobiography of John Adams*

My children were *growing up without my care* in their education, and all my emoluments as a member of Congress for four years had not been sufficient to pay a laboring man on a farm.

—After four years of service to the Continental Congress, 1777

The oldest has given decided proofs of great talents, and there is not a youth his age whose reputation is higher for abilities, or whose character is fairer in point of morals of conduct. The youngest is as fine a youth as either of the three, if a spice of fun in his composition should not lead him astray. Charles wins the heart, as usual, and is the most a gentleman of them all.

—*Writing to his daughter, Nabby, about his three sons John Quincy, Thomas, and Charles*

Let them revere nothing but religion, morality and liberty.

—In a letter to Abigail, concerning their sons

On
the first son, and eventual president, John Quincy Adams.

A taste for literature and a turn for business, united in the same person, never fails to make a great man.

—In a letter to John Quincy

You came into life with advantages which will disgrace you if your success is mediocre . . . And if you do not rise to the head of your country, it will be owing to your own laziness and slovenliness.

—In a discussion with John Quincy

Amidst your Ardour for Greek and Latin I hope you will not forget your mother Tongue. Read Somewhat in the English Poets every day. . . . You will never be alone, with a Poet in your Poket. You will never have an idle Hour.

—In a letter to John Quincy, May 14, 1781

Let the human mind loose. It must be loose. It will be loose. Superstition and dogmatism cannot confine it.

—In a letter to his son, John Quincy, November 13, 1816

No man who ever held the office of President would congratulate a friend on obtaining it. He will make one man ungrateful, and a hundred men his enemies, for every office he can bestow.

—In a letter to John Quincy, upon his election as president, dated 1824

All my hopes are in him, both for my family and my country.

—In a letter to Abigail, regarding John Quincy, 1794

I have often thought he has more prudence at 27 than his father at 58.

—In a letter to Abigail, regarding John Quincy, 1794

On
son, Thomas Adams.

*P*ublic business, my son, must always be done by somebody. It will be done by somebody or other. If wise men decline it, others will not; if honest men refuse it, others will not.

> —In a letter to Thomas after he expressed
> an interest in public office

*M*y advice to my children is to maintain an independent character.
> —In a letter to Thomas

A young man should weigh well his plans.
> —In a letter to Thomas

He is a delightful little fellow. I love him too much.
—In a letter to Abigail, describing Charles, 1780

The four quotes that follow are all from letters to Abigail.

The best Thing We can do, the greatest Respect We can show to the Memory of our departed Friend, is to copy into Our own Lives, those Virtues which in her Lifetime rendered her the Object of our Esteem, Love and Admiration. I must confess I ever felt a Veneration for her, which seems increased by the News of her Translation

—Referring to the passing of his mother-in-law in a letter to Abigail, October 29, 1775

Is there no way for two friendly souls to converse together, although the bodies are 400 miles off. Yes, by letter. But I want a better communication. I want to hear you think, or to see your thoughts.

—In a letter to Abigail, while attending the Continental Congress, 1776

Early Youth is the Time, to learn the Arts and Sciences, and especially to correct the Ear, and the Imagination, by forming a Style. I wish you would think of forming the Taste, and judgment of your Children, now, before any unchaste Sounds have fastened on their Ears, and before any Affectation, or Vanity, is settled on their Minds, upon the pure Principles of Nature ….Musick is a great Advantage, for Style depends in Part upon a delicate Ear.

—In a letter to Abigail, July 7, 1776

I must study politics and war, that our sons may have liberty to study mathematics and philosophy. Our sons ought to study mathematics and philosophy, geography, natural history and naval architecture, navigation, commerce and agriculture in order to give their children a right to study painting, poetry, music, architecture, statuary, tapestry and porcelain.

—In a letter to Abigail, dated 1780

From an advice-filled letter
**to two grandsons, George Washington
and John II.**

Be upon your guard. Remember your youth and inexperience, your total Ignorance of the great World, be always modest, ingenuous, teachable, never assuming or forward, treat all People with respect; preserve the Character of youthful Americans, let nothing unbecoming ever escape your lips or your Behaviour. You have Characters to Support, Reputations to acquire; I may Say, you have the Character of your Country, at least of its Chil[d]hood and youth to Support.

❖

Without a minute Diary, your Travels, will be no better than the flight of Birds, through the Air. They will leave no trace behind them. Whatever you write preserve. I have burned, Bushells of my Silly notes, in fitts of Impatience and humiliation, which I would now give anything to recover. "These fair Creature are thyself." And would be more useful and influential in Self Examination than all the Sermons of the Clergy.

◈

*E*nter into no disputes, upon public affairs, national or European. Say you are too young, too inexperienced, too little read, and too ill informed, to hazard your Judgment on any of these great Things. Leave to your Father the Interests and honor of your Country. There they will be Safe. Be not provoked by any misrepresentations of your Country. This is a hard Lesson but you must learn it.

—In a letter to grandsons George Washington Adams
and John Adams II, May 3, 1815

◈

About the place Adams called "home."

As much as I converse with sages and heroes, they have very little of my love and admiration. I long for rural and domestic scene, for the warbling of birds and the prattling of my children.

—In a letter to Abigail, March 16, 1777

New England has in many Respects the Advantage of every other Colony in America, and indeed of every other Part of the World, that I know any Thing of.

—In a letter to Abigail, October 29, 1775

There live, there to die, there to lay my bones, and there to plant one of my sons in the profession of law and the practices of agriculture, like his father.

—Speaking of his hometown of Braintree,
before returning there in 1788; the son
he wished to "plant" in law was John Quincy

John Adams's autobiography is part of the Adams Family Papers, now held by the Massachusetts Historical Society. The manuscript is 440 pages long.

Ten

YOUR BENIGN INFLUENCE:
IN THE WORDS OF ABIGAIL ADAMS

John Adams sometimes sent conflicting message to his loving wife, Abigail. For example, in 1776 there was the compliment, "I think you shine as a stateswoman." Then, three years later, he tried to protect her from the ugliness of the world: "I must not write a word to you about politics, because you are a woman." History shows that Abigail understood politics and even if she deserves sympathy for the familial sacrifices she made, it would be a mistake to underestimate her intellect. In many regards, she was her husband's equal.

As proof, there are words of warning that she shared with Adams. First, "Remember the Ladies, and be more generous and favorable to them than your ancestors." In addition, "Do not put such unlimited power into the hands of the husbands. Remember all men would be tyrants if they could." It goes without saying that the nation's second president was smart enough to heed his First Lady.

Born on November 22, 1744, Abigail passed away seven years before her son was sworn in as president. She was the first First Lady to live in the White House and one of America's original feminists. She earned her keep as a manager of the family farm and finances.

It is mostly through her correspondence with Adams that we know not only of their relationship, but of the hardships faced by them and other revolutionaries of the time. Much as Adams could be honest about the low points of his life, Abigail portrayed her own life with a truthful quill.

"Great necessities call out great virtues," she wrote. With wise words like that it is easy to agree that her quotations are as worthy of attention as any of the founding fathers.

In 1969, the National Women's Hall of Fame opened its doors in Seneca Falls, New York. Seven years later, Abigail Adams was inducted based on her efforts for equality, one example being her "Remember the Ladies" letter to John. She is also recognized for her accomplishments as the wife of the first ambassador to Great Britain, the second First Lady, and the mother of the sixth president.

If I was sure your absence to day was occasioned, by what it generally is, either to wait upon Company, or promote some good work, I freely confess my Mind would be much more at ease than at present it is. Yet this uneasiness does not arise from any apprehension of Slight or neglect, but a fear least you are indisposed, for that you said should be your only hindrance. Humanity obliges us to be affected with the distresses and Miserys of our fellow creatures. Friendship is a band yet stronger, which causes us to [feel] with greater tenderness the afflictions of our Friends.

—In a letter to John, August 11, 1763

You was *pleas'd* to say that the receipt of a letter from your Diana always gave you pleasure. Whether this was designed for a complement, (a commodity I acknowledg that you very seldom deal in) or as a real truth, you best know. Yet if I was to judge of a certain persons Heart, by what upon the like occasion passess through a cabinet of my own, I should be apt to suspect it as a truth. And why may I not? when I have often been tempted to believe; that they were both cast in the same mould, only with this difference, that yours was made, with a harder mettle, and therefore is less liable to an impression.

—In a letter to John, September 12, 1763

I know you are a critical observer, and your judgment of people generally plases me. Sometimes you know, I think you too severe, and that you do not make quite so many allowances as Humane Nature requires, but perhaps this may be oweing to my unacquainedness with the World.

—In a letter to John, April 13, 1764

I think I write to you every Day. Shall not I make my Letters very cheep; don't you light your pipe with them? I care not if you do, tis a pleasure to me to write, yet I wonder I write to you with so little restraint, for as a critick I fear you more than any other person on Earth, and tis the only character, in which I ever did, or ever will fear you. What say you? Do you approve of that Speach? Dont you think me a Courageous Being? Courage is a laudable, a Glorious Virtue in your Sex, why not in mine? (For my part, I think you ought to applaud me for mine.)

—In a letter to John, April 16, 1764

Sunday seems a more Lonesome Day to me than any other when you are absent, For tho I may be compared to those climates which are deprived of the Sun half the Year, yet upon a Sunday you commonly afforded us your benign influence.

—IN A LETTER TO JOHN, SEPTEMBER 14, 1767

Alas! How many snow banks divide thee and me....

—In a letter to John, December 1773

You cannot be, I know, nor do I wish to see you, an inactive spectator. . . .We have too many high sounding words, and too few actions that correspond with them.

—In a letter to John, 1774

I am very impatient to receive a letter from you. You indulged me so much in that Way in your last absence, that I now think I have a right to hear as often from you as you have leisure and opportunity to write. I hear that Mr. Adams wrote to his Son and the Speaker to his Lady, but perhaps you did not know of the opportunity.

—In a letter to John, September 2, 1774

I wish most sincerely there was not a Slave in the province. It allways appeard a most iniquitious Scheme to me—fight ourselfs for what we are daily robbing and plundering from those who have as good a right to freedom as we have. You know my mind upon this Subject.

—In a letter to John, September 22, 1774

I dare not express to you at 300 hundred miles distance how ardently I long for your return. I have some very miserly Wishes; and cannot consent to your spending one hour in Town till at least I have had you 12. The Idea plays about my Heart, unnerves my hand whilst I write, awakens all the tender sentiments that years have encreased and matured, and which when with me every day was dispensing to you.

—IN A LETTER TO JOHN, OCTOBER 16, 1774

I feard much for your Health when you went away. I must intreat you to be as careful as you can consistant with the Duty you owe your Country. That consideration alone prevaild with me to consent to your departure, in a time so perilous and so hazardous to your family, and with a body so infirm as to require the tenderest care and nursing. I wish you may be supported and devinely assisted in this most important crisis when the fate of Empires depend upon your wisdom and conduct. I greatly rejoice to hear of your union, and determination to stand by us.

—In a letter to John, June 16, 1775

The race is not to the swift, nor the battle to the strong; but the God of Israel is He that giveth strength and power unto His people. Trust in Him at all times, ye people, pour out your hearts before him; God is a refuge for us.

—In a letter to John, June 18, 1775

*C*harleston is laid in ashes. The battle began upon our entrenchments upon Bunker's Hill, Saturday morning about 3 o'clock, and has not ceased yet, and it is now three o'clock Sabbath afternoon. It is expected they will come out over the Neck tonight, and a dreadful battle must ensue. Almighty God, cover the heads of our countrymen, and be a shield to our dear friends...

—In a letter to John, June 18, 1775

The Day; perhaps the decisive Day is come on which the fate of America depends. My bursting Heart must find vent at my pen. I have just heard that our dear Friend Dr. Warren is no more but fell gloriously fighting for his Country — saying better to die honourably in the field than ignominiously hang upon the Gallows. Great is our Loss. He has distinguished himself in every engagement, by his courage and fortitude, by animating the Soldiers and leading them on by his own example. A particuliar account of these dreadful, but I hope Glorious Days will be transmitted you, no doubt in the exactest manner.

—In a letter to John, June 20, 1775

I want you to be more perticuliar. Does every Member feel for us? Can they realize what we suffer? And can they believe with what patience and fortitude we endure the conflict — nor do we even tremble at the frowns of power.

—In a letter to John, regarding the Continental Congress and their stance on women, June 22, 1775

Your Description of the Distresses of the worthy Inhabitants of Boston, and the other Sea Port Towns, is enough to melt an Heart of Stone. Our Consolation must be this, my dear, that Cities may be rebuilt, and a People reduced to Poverty, may acquire fresh Property: But a Constitution of Government once changed from Freedom, can never be restored. Liberty once lost is lost forever. When the People once surrender their share in the Legislature, and their Right of defending the Limitations upon the Government, and of resisting every Encroachment upon them, they can never regain it...

—In a letter to John, July 7, 1775

You will think me melancholy. Tis true I am much affected with the distress'd Scenes around me but I have some Anxietyes upon my mind which I do not think it prudent to mention at present to any one. Perhaps when I hear from you, I may in my next Letter tell you. In the mean time I wish you would tell me whether the intercepted Letters have reachd Phyladelphia and what affect they have there. There is a most infamous versification of them I hear sent out. I have not been able to get it.

—IN A LETTER TO JOHN, SEPTEMBER 17, 1775

In past years small has been my portion of the Bitter Cup in comparison with many others. But there is now prepairing for me I fear, a large draught thereof. May I be enabled to submit with patience and resignation to the rod and him who hath appointed it, knowing it is directed by unerring wisdom.

—In a letter to John, September 29, 1775

Forgive me then, for thus dwelling upon a subject sweet to me, but I fear painfull to you. O how I have long'd for your Bosom to pour forth my sorrows there, and find a healing Balm, but perhaps that has been denied me that I might be led to a higher and a more permamant consolater who has bid us call upon him in the day of trouble.

—In a letter to John, October 9, 1775

A *patriot without religion* in my estimation is as great a paradox as an honest Man without the fear of God. Is it possible that he whom no moral obligations bind, can have any real Good Will towards Men? Can he be a patriot who, by an openly vicious conduct, is undermining the very bonds of Society? . . . The Scriptures tell us "righteousness exalteth a Nation."

—In a letter to Mercy Warren, November 1775

Let us separate, they are unworthy to be our brethren.

—In a letter to John, after he refused to sign the Olive Branch Petition which called for reconciliation with Great Britain, November 12, 1775

I *am more and more convinced* that man is a dangerous creature; and that power, whether vested in many or a few, is ever grasping, and like the grave, cries "Give, give!"

—In a letter to John, November 27, 1775

Tis a fortnight to Night since I wrote you a line
during which, I have been confined with the jaundice,
Rhumatism and a most violent cold; I yesterday took a puke
which has releived me, and I feel much better to day. Many,
very many people who have had the dysentery, are now afflicted both with the jaundice and Rhumatisim, some it has
left in Hecticks, some in dropsies.

—In a letter to John, November 27, 1775

The reins of government have been so long slackened, that I fear the people will not quietly submit to those
restraints which are necessary for the peace and security of
the community.

—In a letter to John, November 27, 1775

If particular care and attention is not paid to the Ladies we are determined to foment a Rebellion, and will not hold ourselves bound by any Laws in which we have no voice, or Representation.

—In a letter to John, March 31, 1776

You inquire of whether *I am making Salt peter.* I have not yet attempted it, but after Soap making believe I shall make the experiment. I find as much as I can do to manufacture cloathing for my family who which would else be Naked.

—In a letter to John, March 31 - April 5, 1776

I cannot say that I think you are very generous to the ladies; for, whilst you are proclaiming peace and good-will to men, emancipating all nations, you insist upon retaining an absolute power over wives.

—In a letter to John, May 7, 1776

By yesterdays post *I received two Letters* dated 3 and 4 of July and tho your Letters never fail to give me pleasure, be the subject what it will, yet it was greatly heightned by the prospect of the future happiness and glory of our Country; nor am I a little Gratified when I reflect that a person so nearly connected with me has had the Honour of being a principal actor, in laying a foundation for its future Greatness. May the foundation of our new constitution, be justice, Truth and Righteousness. Like the wise Mans house may it be founded upon those Rocks and then neither storms or temptests will overthrow it. I cannot but feel sorry that some of the most Manly Sentiments in the Declaration are Expunged from the printed coppy. Perhaps wise reasons induced it.

—In a letter to John, July 14, 1776

There are perticuliar times when I feel such an uneasiness, such a restlessness, as neither company, Books, family Cares or any other thing will remove, my Pen is my only pleasure, and writing to you the composure of my mind.

—IN A LETTER TO JOHN, SEPTEMBER 23, 1776

I regret the trifling narrow contracted education of the females of my own country.

—In a letter to John, June 30, 1778

These are times in which a genius would wish to live. It is not in the still calm of life, or the repose of a pacific station, that great characters are formed.

—In a letter to John Quincy, January 19, 1780

...a little like getting out of the frying pan and into the fire.

—In a letter to John, describing the prospects of continuing their life in politics, upon returning to the U.S. in 1788

I *think of my poor dear and pity him.*

—Describing Adams's wait to find out if he would be vice president, in a letter to Mary Cranch, 1788

I am fearful of touching upon political subjects. Yet perhaps there is no person who feels more interested in them.

—Describing the conflicting feelings she had during Adams's first year as vice president, 1790

He has ever sustained the character of
the independent freeman of America.

—In a letter to daughter Nabby, 1791

I am happy to learn that the only fault in
your political character, and one which has always
given me uneasiness, is wearing away. I mean a
certain irritability which has sometimes thrown you
off your guard.

—In a letter to John, 1793

He was no man's enemy, but his own.

—Writing about Charles upon his death, 1800

Mr. Adams held to his faith in land as true wealth.

—In a conversation with Cotton Tufts,
explaining why John and she hadn't invested in
government securities

In their old age, John and Abigail were referred to as the
"grandparents of their country."

Eleven

AMERICA'S FIRST AMBASSADOR:
ABOUT JOHN ADAMS

The following quotes speak for themselves. John Adams was a widely respected leader and a bonafide political philosopher. He was a well-respected negotiator and as the icing on the cake, he got to see his son live up to all of his expectations when John Quincy was elected the sixth president of the United States. Surrounded as he was by sharp minds, it should be no surprise to find that there were plenty of quotes about John Adams worthy of inclusion in this book. As a bonus, at the end of the chapter are some self-evaluations, delivered more often than not in the form of a diary entry. These quotes are a wonderful opportunity to look into the mirror through the great man's eyes. He was an astute judge of character, that's for sure. He understood his own penchant for oversocializing and was forthright when it came to his financial concerns. In reflecting on his situation, Adams allowed future generations the opportunity to see what the founding fathers were really risking with every step they took away from the British.

John Adams loved the state of Massachusetts. He was born in Braintree, graduated from Harvard University, practiced law and for a time kept a house in Boston, retired in Braintree (which eventually came to be called Quincy), and was buried there.

I have heard of one Mr. Adams but who is the other?

—King George III, referring to Adams's second cousin, Samuel Adams

John Adams, America's first Ambassador, said to my ancestor, King George III, that it was his desire to help with the restoration of "the old good nature and the old good humor between our peoples."

—Queen Elizabeth II

John Adams is a man of the shortest of what is called middle size in England, strong and tight-made, rather inclining to fat, of a complexion that bespeaks a warmer climate than Massachusetts is supposed, a countenance which bespeaks rather reflection than imagination.

—William Alexander, British spy

He has, I believe, a keen temper which if he can command thoroughly, will be a great merit.

—William Alexander

From a Massachusetts Centinel story
**about the parade to celebrate Adams's return
from Europe.**

*T*he bells in several churches rang during the remainder of the day—every countenance wore the expressions of joy.

—MAY 18, 1817

*M*erit must be conspicuously great when it can thus call forth the voluntary honors of a free and enlightened people. But the attentions shown on this occasion were not merely honorary—they were the tribute of gratitude due to a man who after retirement from trials and services which were of 18 years unremitted continuance, hath again stepped forth to endeavor to establish and perpetuate that independence . . . and which his exertions have so greatly contributed to produce.

It came from *the heart of a tried patriot*, and was addressed to the hearts of patriots alone.

—From an article in the *Gazette of the United States*
about a May 16, 1797 speech, delivered to Congress,
about the possibility of war with France

No man better merited than Mr. John Adams to hold a most conspicuous place in the design. He was the pillar of its support on the floor of Congress, its ablest advocate and defender against the multifarious assaults encountered.

—THOMAS JEFFERSON, DESCRIBING ADAMS'S SUPPORT
FOR THE *DECLARATION OF INDEPENDENCE*

The Colossus of that Congress—the great pillar of support to the Declaration of Independence, and its ablest advocate and champion on the floor of the House.

—Thomas Jefferson on Adams and his role in the drafting and adoption of the Declaration of Independence

His power of thought and expression . . . moved us from our seats.

—Thomas Jefferson

No man on earth pays more cordial homage to your words or wishes more fervently your happiness.

—Thomas Jefferson, upon learning of Adams's election as vice president

We must bend then before the gale, and try to hold fast ourselves by some plank of the wreck. God send us all a safe deliverance, and to yourself every other species and degree of happiness.

—Thomas Jefferson, January 24, 1814

He means well for his country, is always an honest man, often a wise one, but sometimes, in some things, absolutely out of his senses.

—Benjamin Franklin

The man to whom the country is most indebted for the great measure of independency.

—Richard Stockton, lawyer and signer of the *Declaration of Independence*

This illustrious patriot has not his superior, scarcely his equal for abilities and virtue on the whole continent of America.

—*Benjamin Rush*

[John Adams was] a real American in principle and conduct.

—Benjamin Rush

I expected to be inspired with a painful awe, but strange to tell, every idea of distance was immediately banished.

—Judith Sargent Murray, feminist and author who wrote under the pseudonym The Gleaner, after meeting Adams in 1788

Adams strove for a religion based on a common sense sort of reasonableness.

—Robert B. Everett

It is universally admitted that Mr. Adams is a man of incorruptible integrity, and that the resources of his own mind are equal to the duties of his station.

—From an article in the *Aurora*, covering his inauguration on March 4, 1797

By his opinions, advice, and recommendations, he has, I believe, in his power to do as much, perhaps the most, towards establishing her character as a respectable nation of any man in America.

—From his daughter Nabby

...and shall he retire from the world and bury himself amongst his books, and live only for himself? No—I wish it not.

—From his daughter Nabby

Then, appointed *the first American minister* to Britain, Adams presented his credentials to George III in 1785, noting his pride in "having the distinguished honor to be the first (ex-colonial subject) to stand in your Majesty's royal presence in a diplomatic character."

—RALPH KETCHAM, HISTORIAN AND AUTHOR

Although his own presidency (1797–1801) was a troubled one, Adams made uniquely important contributions during his term as chief executive. He managed orderly transitions of power at both the beginning and the end of his administration, and he gave the government stability by continuing most of the practices established under Washington.

—Ralph Ketcham

Ninety years old at his death, Adams was revered by his countrymen not only as one of the founding fathers but also as a plain, honest man who personified the best of what the nation could hope of its citizens and leaders.

—Ralph Ketcham

[John Adams was] the greatest political thinker whom America has yet produced.

—*Harold Laski, political scientist*

Madison was the great intellectual . . . Jefferson the unquenchable idealist . . . and Franklin the most charming and versatile genius . . . but Adams is the most captivating founding father on most counts.

—ROBERT A. RUTLAND, HISTORIAN AND AUTHOR

That he had pressed doggedly for a greater part in the war by the French navy would stand as one of his proudest efforts . . .

—David McCullough, historian and author, discussing Adams's efforts during the Revolutionary War

With his success obtaining Dutch loans at the critical hour of the Revolution, he felt, as did others, that he had truly saved his country.

—David McCullough

He would have preferred more power in the presidency than provided—particularly the authority to make presidential appointments without Senate approval. But of greater concern was the absence of a bill of rights, in the spirit of what he had written for the constitution of Massachusetts.

—DAVID MCCULLOUGH

Adams was utterly opposed to slavery

and the slave trade and, like [Benjamin] Rush, favored a gradual emancipation of all slaves.

—David McCullough

Adams in his own words.

I soon perceived a growing Curiosity, a Love of Books and a fondness for Study, which dissipated all my Inclination for Sports, and even for the Society of the Ladies. I read forever, but without much method, and with very little Choice. I got my Lessons regularly and performed my recitations without Censure. Mathematicks and natural Phylosophy attracted the most of my Attention, which I have since regretted, because I was destined to a Course of Life, in which these Sciences have been of little Use, and the Classicks would have been of great Importance. I owe to this however perhaps some degree of Patience of Investigation, which I might not otherwise have obtained.

—From *The Adams Papers: Diary and Autobiography of John Adams*

I was of an amorous disposition and very early from ten or eleven Years of Age, was very fond of the Society of females. I had my favorites among the young Women and spent many of my Evenings in their Company and this disposition although controlled for seven Years after my Entrance into College returned and engaged me too much till I was married.

—From *The Adams Papers: Diary and Autobiography of John Adams*

I am constantly forming, but never executing good resolutions.

—From a diary entry, February 11, 1756

I take great Pleasure, in viewing and examining the magnificent Prospects of Nature, that lie before us in this Town. If I cast my Eyes one Way, I am entertained with the Savage and unsightly appearance of naked woods and leafless Forests. In another place a chain of broken and irregular mountains, throws my mind into a pleasing kind of astonishment.

—Describing Braintree in a diary entry,
February 11, 1756

◆

A charming morning. My Classmate Gardner drank Tea with me. Spent an Hour in the beginning of the evening at Major Gardiners, where it was thought that the design of Christianity was not to make men good Riddle Solvers or good mystery mongers, but good men, good majestrates and good Subjects, good Husbands and good Wives, good Parents and good Children, good masters and good servants.

—From a diary entry, February 18, 1756

◆

In the Years 1766 and 1767 my Business increased, as my Reputation spread, I got Money and bought Books and Land. I had heard my father say that he never knew a Piece of Land run away or break, and I was too much enamoured with Books, to spend many thoughts upon Speculation on Money. I was often solicited to lend Money and sometimes complied upon Land Security: but I was more intent on my Business than on my Profits, or I should have laid the foundation of a better Estate.

—From *The Adams Papers: Diary and Autobiography of John Adams*

◈

To divert men minds from subjects of vain curiosity, or unprofitable science, to the useful, as well as entertaining speculations of agriculture; to eradicate the Gothic and pernicious principles of private revenge that have been lately spread among my countrymen, to the debasement of their character, and to the frequent violation of the public peace, and to recommend a careful attention to political measures, and a candid manner of reasoning about them, instead of abusive insolence or uncharitable imputations upon men and characters, has, since I first undertook the employment of entertaining the public, been my constant and invariable view.

—In a published letter, August 29, 1768

◈

In 1769... The House I lived in, was to be sold: I had not sufficient confidence in the Stability of any Thing, to purchase it, and I therefore removed to a house in cold Lane: where I lost a Child a Daughter, whose name was Susana, and where in 1770 my Son Charles was born.

—From *The Adams Papers: Diary and Autobiography of John Adams*

◈

*H*ow long I shall be able to stay in the City, I know not; if my Health should again decline, I must return to Braintree and renounce the Town entirely. I hope however to be able to stay there many Years! To this End I must remember Temperance, Exercise and Peace of Mind. Above all Things I must avoid politicks, Political Clubbs, Town Meetings, General Court, &c. &c. &c. I must ride frequently to Braintree to inspect my Farm, and when in Boston must spend my Evenings in my Office, or with my Family, and with as little Company as possible.

—Musing over his upcoming move to Boston in a diary entry, November 21, 1772

I never engaged in public affairs for my own interest, pleasure, envy, jealousy, avarice or ambition, or even the desire of fame.

—In a published letter, August 29, 1775

*M*y Smattering of Mathematicks enabled me afterwards at Auteuil in France to go, with my eldest Son, through a Course of Geometry, Algebra and several Branches of the Sciences, with a degree of pleasure that amply rewarded me for all my time and pains.

—From *The Adams Papers: Diary and Autobiography of John Adams*

*S*pent the Morning in translating with my Son the Carmen Seculare, and the Notes. There is a Feebleness and a Languor in my Nature. My Mind and Body both partake of this Weakness. By my Physical Constitution, I am but an ordinary Man.

—From a diary entry, April 26, 1779

*I*n one of my common Walks, along the Edgeware
Road, there are fine Meadows, or Squares of grass
Land belonging to a noted Cow keeper. These Plotts are plenti-
fully manured. There are on the Side of the Way, several heaps
of Manure, an hundred Loads perhaps in each heap. I have
carefully examined them and find them composed of Straw,
and dung from the Stables and Streets of London, mud, Clay,
or Marl, dug out of the Ditch, along the Hedge, and Turf, Sward
cutt up, with Spades, hoes, and shovels in the Road. This is laid
in vast heaps to mix. With narrow hoes they cutt it down at
each End, and with shovels throw it into a new heap, in order to
divide it and mix it more effectually. I have attended to the Operation, as I walked, for some time. This may be good manure,
but is not equal to mine, which I composed in similar heaps
upon my own Farm . . .

—From a diary entry, written in London, July 8, 1786

*P*opularity was never my mistress, nor as I ever, or shall I ever be a popular man.

—In a letter to James Warren, 1787

◈

I hate speeches, messages, addresses, proclamations and such affected, constrained things. I hate levees and drawing rooms. I hate to speak to 1,000 people to whom I have nothing to say. Yet all this I can do.

—In a letter to Abigail, regarding what it would take
for him to win the presidency, 1796

◈

*I*n conformity to the fashion I drank this Morning and Yesterday Morning, about a Jill of Cyder. It seems to do me good, by diluting and dissolving the Phlegm or the Bile in the Stomach.

—From a diary entry, July 26, 1796

*O*f all the Summers of my Life, this has been the freest from Care, Anxiety and Vexation to me. The Sickness of Mrs. A. excepted. My Health has been better, the Season fruitful, my farm was conducted. Alas! what may happen to reverse all this? But it is folly to anticipate evils, and madness to create imaginary ones.

—From a diary entry, August 4, 1796

*B*athing my Feet and drinking balm Tea, last night composed me somewhat, and I hope the Rhubarb and Salt of Wormwood I took this Morning will carry off my Complaints: but the Pain in my head and the burnings in my hands and feet were so like the Commencement of my Fevers of 1781 at Amsterdam and of 1783 at Paris and Auteuil, that I began to be allarmed.

—From a diary entry, August 24. 1796

I think to christen my Place by the Name of Peace field, in commemoration of the Peace which I assisted in making in 1783, of the thirteen Years Peace and Neutrality which I have contributed to preserve, and of the constant Peace and Tranquility which I have enjoyed in this Residence.

—From a diary entry, September 8, 1796

You talk of my enemies, but I assure you I have none.

—Replying to John Trumbull's concern that southerners did not like Adams

*M*ay Heaven assist me, for at present I see nothing but clouds and darkness before me.

— Writing about his concern for his finances and for his ability to serve as the nation's first vice president

To be wholly overlooked, and to know it, are intolerable.

—Writing about his role as vice president

❖

Oh! That I could have a home! Rolling, rolling, rolling, till I am very nearly rolling into the bosom of Mother Earth.

—Commenting on his return to Braintree after four years as president, as well as years abroad as U.S. ambassador

❖

I desire no other inscription over my gravestone-than: "Here lies John Adams, who took upon himself the responsibility of peace with France in the year 1800."

—Stated after negotiating a treaty with France in 1800

*A*s the Lives of Phylosophers, Statesmen or Historians written by them selves have generally been suspected of Vanity, and therefore few People have been able to read them without disgust; there is no reason to expect that any Sketches I may leave of my own Times would be received by the Public with any favour, or read by individuals with much interest.

—From *The Adams Papers: Diary and Autobiography of John Adams*

I must be within scent of the sea.

—In a letter to Abigail, responding to her suggestion of a move from Massachusetts to Vermont

The last words John Adams uttered, before passing away on July 4, 1826, were, "Thomas Jefferson lives." But Jefferson died the very same day. This was the 50th anniversary of the signing of their Declaration of Independence; John Adams was ninety years old and Thomas Jefferson was eighty-one. The president at the time of Adams's and Jefferson's death was Adams's son, John Quincy Adams. Also of note is the fact that Adams held the distinction of being the longest living ex-president, until Ronald Reagan set a new record in 2001.

Closing

A life ends, but if it was a life lived to the fullest then it is a life that will live on in story. Or history, as is the case with someone like John Adams.

Despite his role as attorney, rebel, Continental Congressman, ambassador, vice president, president of the Senate, president of the nation, father of a president, and confidant of Thomas Jefferson, Adams stood in the shadows of others. As a young man, he admitted feeling slighted at times. In diary entries and letters to Abigail, he would often get a complaint off of his chest and then criticize himself for feeling self-pity. No man is perfect and if this was as faulty as Adams's character got, it would seem a weakness everyone could live with.

Adams made his name during a precarious time in the nation's history. The revolution was no sure thing, and this is sometimes lost in a reverie of fireworks and fife and drum corps. Rare is the time that a modern American imagines what it would be like to miss the most important ten years of your children's life so that you can negotiate peace with your country's former colonizer. Rare is the time that a modern American imagines the internal conflict a founding father must have felt when offered a political position with no known salary. These are not glorious thoughts, but they are thoughts that Adams had to contemplate. And in reading about them here, his story certainly becomes more personal; the story of America's birth becomes more real.

Some of the quotations serve a different purpose, though, shedding light on other famous leaders of the time. Adams had relationships with people like George Washington, Thomas Jefferson, and Benjamin Franklin. Abigail was his wife and a fantastic First Lady. Samuel was his cousin and a rebel whose reputation spread before anyone even knew who John Adams was. John Quincy was his son and the sixth president of the United States. Adams was surrounded by greatness for much of his life and in studying that life, a lot can be learned about the most important era in American history. It was a time for rebels and statesmen, democrats and capitalists, philosophers and funny guys. It was a time for patriots like John Adams.

Sources

<http://www25.uua.org/uuhs/duub/articles/johnadams.html>
Retrieved October 5, 2007.

Cappon, Lester J. (Ed.). (1988). *The Adams-Jefferson Letters: The Complete Correspondence Between Thomas Jefferson and Abigail and John Adams.* North Carolina: University of North Carolina Press.

Diggins, John Patrick (Ed.). (2004). *The Portable John Adams.* New York: Penguin Classics.

Hogan, Margaret A. & Taylor, C. James. (Eds.) (2007). *My Dearest Friend: Letters of Abigail and John Adams.* Boston: Belknap Press.

McCullough, David (2001). *John Adams.* New York: Simon & Schuster.

<http://oregonstate.edu/instruct/phl302/philosophers/hume.html>
Retrieved October 5, 2007.

<http://www.sparknotes.com/biography/johnadams/>
Retrieved October 5, 2007.

<http://www.utm.edu/research/iep/l/locke.htm>
　　Retrieved October 5, 2007.

<http://www.whitehouse.gov/history/presidents/ja2.html>
　　Retrieved October 5, 2007.